Afghans by the Alphabet

Designs by Anne Halliday

Leisure Arts Inc. • Maumelle Arkansas

TABLE OF CONTENT

Angels Among Us

Finished Size: 53" x $68^1/_2$"
(134.5 cm x 174 cm)

MATERIALS
Worsted Weight Yarn:
White - 42 ounces, 2,280 yards
(1,190 grams, 2,085 meters)
Blue - 35 ounces, 1,900 yards
(990 grams, 1,737.5 meters)
Crochet hook, size I (5.5 mm) **or** size needed for gauge

GAUGE: In pattern,
(sc, ch 1) 8 times = $4^1/_4$" (10.75 cm);
14 rows = 4" (10 cm)

Gauge Swatch: $4^1/_2$"w x 4"h
(11.5 cm x 10 cm)
With Blue, ch 18.
Rows 1-9: Work same as Afghan Body.
Rows 10-14: Repeat Rows 8 and 9 twice, then repeat Row 8 once **more**.

Each row is worked across length of Afghan. When joining yarn and finishing off, leave an 8" (20.5 cm) end to be worked into fringe.

STITCH GUIDE

CLUSTER
Ch 3, YO, insert hook in third ch from hook, YO and pull up a loop, YO and draw through 2 loops on hook, YO, insert hook in same ch, YO and pull up a loop, YO and draw through 2 loops on hook, YO and draw through all 3 loops on hook.

AFGHAN BODY

With Blue, ch 258.

Row 1 (Right side)**:** Sc in second ch from hook, ★ ch 1, skip next ch, sc in next ch; repeat from ★ across; finish off: 129 sc and 128 ch-1 sps.

Note: Loop a short piece of yarn around any stitch to mark Row 1 as **right** side.

Row 2: With **wrong** side facing, join White with sc in first sc ***(see Joining With Sc, page 68)***; ★ work Cluster, skip next sc and next ch-1 sp, sc in next st; repeat from ★ across; finish off: 64 Clusters and 65 sc.

Row 3: With **right** side facing, join Blue with sc in first sc; ★ ch 1, working **behind** next Cluster ***(Fig. 4, page 69)***, dc in skipped sc one row **below**, ch 1, sc in next sc; repeat from ★ across; finish off: 129 sts and 128 ch-1 sps.

Row 4: With **wrong** side facing, join White with sc in first sc; ch 1, skip next ch-1 sp, sc in next st, ★ work Cluster, skip next sc and next ch-1 sp, sc in next st; repeat from ★ across to last ch-1 sp, ch 1, skip last ch-1 sp, sc in last sc; finish off: 63 Clusters and 66 sc.

Row 5: With **right** side facing, join Blue with sc in first sc; ★ ch 1, sc in next sc, ch 1, working **behind** next Cluster, dc in skipped sc one row **below**; repeat from ★ across to last 2 sc, (ch 1, sc in next sc) twice; finish off: 129 sts and 128 ch-1 sps.

Rows 6 and 7: Repeat Rows 2 and 3.

Row 8: With **wrong** side facing, join White with sc in first sc; ★ ch 1, skip next ch-1 sp, sc in next st; repeat from ★ across; finish off: 129 sc and 128 ch-1 sps.

Row 9: With **right** side facing, join Blue with sc in first sc; (ch 1, sc in next sc) across; finish off.

Rows 10 and 11: Repeat Rows 8 and 9.

Row 12: With **wrong** side facing, join White with sc in first sc; (ch 1, sc in next sc) 5 times, ★ † (work Cluster, skip next sc and next ch-1 sp, sc in next st) 3 times, (ch 1, skip next ch-1 sp, sc in next st) 6 times, work Cluster, skip next sc and next ch-1 sp, sc in next st †, (ch 1, sc in next sc) 12 times; repeat from ★ 3 times **more**, then repeat from † to † once, (ch 1, sc in next sc) 5 times; finish off: 109 sc, 20 Clusters, and 88 ch-1 sps.

Continued on page 6.

Row 13: With **right** side facing, join Blue with sc in first sc; (ch 1, sc in next sc) 5 times, ★ † ch 1, working **behind** next Cluster, dc in skipped sc one row **below**, (ch 1, sc in next sc) 7 times, (ch 1, working **behind** next Cluster, dc in skipped sc one row **below**, ch 1, sc in next sc) 3 times †, (ch 1, sc in next sc) 12 times; repeat from ★ 3 times **more**, then repeat from † to † once, (ch 1, sc in next sc) 5 times; finish off: 129 sts and 128 ch-1 sps.

Row 14: With **wrong** side facing, join White with sc in first sc; (ch 1, skip next ch-1 sp, sc in next st) 6 times, ★ † (work Cluster, skip next sc and next ch-1 sp, sc in next st) 3 times, (ch 1, skip next ch-1 sp, sc in next st) 4 times, (work Cluster, skip next sc and next ch-1 sp, sc in next st) twice †, (ch 1, skip next ch-1 sp, sc in next st) 12 times; repeat from ★ 3 times **more**, then repeat from † to † once, (ch 1, sc in next sc) 4 times; finish off: 104 sc, 25 Clusters, and 78 ch-1 sps.

Row 15: With **right** side facing, join Blue with sc in first sc; (ch 1, sc in next sc) 4 times, ★ † (ch 1, working **behind** next Cluster, dc in skipped sc one row **below**, ch 1, sc in next sc) twice, (ch 1, sc in next sc) 4 times, (ch 1, working **behind** next Cluster, dc in skipped sc one row **below**, ch 1, sc in next sc) 3 times †, (ch 1, sc in next sc) 12 times; repeat from ★ 3 times **more**, then repeat from † to † once, (ch 1, sc in next sc) 6 times; finish off: 129 sts and 128 ch-1 sps.

Row 16: With **wrong** side facing, join White with sc in first sc; (ch 1, skip next ch-1 sp, sc in next st) 7 times, ★ † (work Cluster, skip next sc and next ch-1 sp, sc in next st) 3 times, (ch 1, skip next ch-1 sp, sc in next st) twice, (work Cluster, skip next sc and next ch-1 sp, sc in next st) 3 times †, (ch 1, skip next ch-1 sp, sc in next st) 12 times; repeat from ★ 3 times **more**, then repeat from † to † once, (ch 1, sc in next sc) 3 times; finish off: 99 sc, 30 Clusters, and 68 ch-1 sps.

Row 17: With **right** side facing, join Blue with sc in first sc; (ch 1, sc in next sc) 3 times, ★ † (ch 1, working **behind** next Cluster, dc in skipped sc one row **below**, ch 1, sc in next sc) 3 times, (ch 1, sc in next sc) twice, (ch 1, working **behind** next Cluster, dc in skipped sc one row **below**, ch 1, sc in next sc) 3 times †, (ch 1, sc in next sc) 12 times; repeat from ★ 3 times **more**, then repeat from † to † once, (ch 1, sc in next sc) 7 times; finish off: 129 sts and 128 ch-1 sps.

Row 18: With **wrong** side facing, join White with sc in first sc; (ch 1, skip next ch-1 sp, sc in next st) 8 times, ★ † (work Cluster, skip next sc and next ch-1 sp, sc in next st) twice, (ch 1, skip next ch-1 sp, sc in next st) twice, (work Cluster, skip next sc and next ch-1 sp, sc in next st) 4 times †, (ch 1, skip next ch-1 sp, sc in next st) 12 times; repeat from ★ 3 times **more**, then repeat from † to † once, (ch 1, sc in next sc) twice; finish off: 99 sc, 30 Clusters, and 68 ch-1 sps.

Row 19: With **right** side facing, join Blue with sc in first sc; (ch 1, sc in next sc) twice, ★ † (ch 1, working **behind** next Cluster, dc in skipped sc one row **below**, ch 1, sc in next sc) 4 times, (ch 1, sc in next sc) twice, (ch 1, working **behind** next Cluster, dc in skipped sc one row **below**, ch 1, sc in next sc) twice †, (ch 1, sc in next sc) 12 times; repeat from ★ 3 times **more**, then repeat from † to † once, (ch 1, sc in next sc) 8 times; finish off: 129 sts and 128 ch-1 sps.

Row 20: With **wrong** side facing, join White with sc in first sc; (ch 1, skip next ch-1 sp, sc in next st) 9 times, ★ † (work Cluster, skip next sc and next ch-1 sp, sc in next st) 7 times †, (ch 1, skip next ch-1 sp, sc in next st) 12 times; repeat from ★ 3 times **more**, then repeat from † to † once, ch 1, sc in last sc; finish off: 94 sc, 35 Clusters, and 58 ch-1 sps.

Row 21: With **right** side facing, join Blue with sc in first sc; ch 1, sc in next sc, ★ † (ch 1, working **behind** next Cluster, dc in skipped sc one row **below**, ch 1, sc in next sc) 7 times †, (ch 1, sc in next sc) 12 times; repeat from ★ 3 times **more**, then repeat from † to † once, (ch 1, sc in next sc) 9 times; finish off: 129 sts and 128 ch-1 sps.

Row 22: With **wrong** side facing, join White with sc in first sc; (ch 1, skip next ch-1 sp, sc in next st) twice, ★ † work Cluster, skip next sc, sc in next sc, ch 1, skip next ch-1 sp, sc in next st, (work Cluster, skip next sc and next ch-1 sp, sc in next st) twice, ch 1, skip next ch-1 sp, sc in next st, (work Cluster, skip next sc and next ch-1 sp, sc in next st) 6 times †, (ch 1, skip next ch-1 sp, sc in next st) 6 times; repeat from ★ 3 times **more**, then repeat from † to † once, (ch 1, sc in next sc) twice; finish off: 84 sc, 45 Clusters, and 38 ch-1 sps.

Row 23: With **right** side facing, join Blue with sc in first sc; (ch 1, sc in next sc) twice, ★ † (ch 1, working **behind** next Cluster, dc in skipped sc one row **below**, ch 1, sc in next sc) 6 times, ch 1, sc in next sc, (ch 1, working **behind** next Cluster, dc in skipped sc one row **below**, ch 1, sc in next sc) twice, ch 1, sc in next sc, ch 1, working **behind** next Cluster, dc in skipped sc one row **below** †, (ch 1, sc in next sc) 7 times; repeat from ★ 3 times **more**, then repeat from † to † once, (ch 1, sc in next sc) 3 times; finish off: 129 sts and 128 ch-1 sps.

Row 24: With **wrong** side facing, join White with sc in first sc; ch 1, sc in next sc, ★ † work Cluster, skip next st and next ch-1 sp, sc in next st, ch 1, sc in next sc, (work Cluster, skip next st and next ch-1 sp, sc in next st) 3 times, ch 1, sc in next dc, (work Cluster, skip next sc and next ch-1 sp, sc in next st) 6 times †, (ch 1, sc in next sc) 4 times; repeat from ★ 3 times **more**, then repeat from † to † once, ch 1, sc in last sc; finish off: 79 sc, 50 Clusters, and 28 ch-1 sps.

Row 25: With **right** side facing, join Blue with sc in first sc; ch 1, sc in next sc, ★ † (ch 1, working **behind** next Cluster, dc in skipped sc one row **below**, ch 1, sc in next sc) 6 times, ch 1, sc in next sc, (ch 1, working **behind** next Cluster, dc in skipped st one row **below**, ch 1, sc in next sc) 3 times, ch 1, sc in next sc, ch 1, working **behind** next Cluster, dc in skipped st one row **below** †, (ch 1, sc in next sc) 5 times; repeat from ★ 3 times **more**, then repeat from † to † once, (ch 1, sc in next sc) twice; finish off: 129 sts and 128 ch-1 sps.

Row 26: With **wrong** side facing, join White with sc in first sc; ch 1, sc in next sc, ★ † work Cluster, skip next dc, sc in next sc, ch 1, sc in next sc, (work Cluster, skip next st and next ch-1 sp, sc in next st) 9 times †, (ch 1, sc in next sc) 5 times; repeat from ★ 3 times **more**, then repeat from † to † once, (ch 1, sc in next sc) twice; finish off: 79 sc, 50 Clusters, and 28 ch-1 sps.

Row 27: With **right** side facing, join Blue with sc in first sc; (ch 1, sc in next sc) twice, ★ † (ch 1, working **behind** next Cluster, dc in skipped st one row **below**, ch 1, sc in next sc) 9 times, ch 1, sc in next sc, ch 1, working **behind** next Cluster, dc in skipped dc one row **below** †, (ch 1, sc in next sc) 6 times; repeat from ★ 3 times **more**, then repeat from † to † once, (ch 1, sc in next sc) twice; finish off: 129 sts and 128 ch-1 sps.

Rows 28 and 29: Repeat Rows 24 and 25.

Rows 30 and 31: Repeat Rows 22 and 23.

Rows 32 and 33: Repeat Rows 20 and 21.

Rows 34 and 35: Repeat Rows 18 and 19.

Rows 36 and 37: Repeat Rows 16 and 17.

Rows 38 and 39: Repeat Rows 14 and 15.

Rows 40 and 41: Repeat Rows 12 and 13.

Rows 42-45: Repeat Rows 8 and 9 twice.

Rows 46-183: Repeat Rows 2-45, 3 times; then repeat Rows 2-7 once **more**.

TRIM

FIRST SIDE

Row 1: With **wrong** side facing, join Blue with sc in first sc on Row 183; ★ ch 1, skip next ch-1 sp, sc in next st; repeat from ★ across; finish off.

Row 2: With **right** side facing, join Blue with slip st in first sc; slip st in next ch-1 sp, (ch 1, slip st in next ch-1 sp) across to last sc, slip st in last sc; finish off.

SECOND SIDE

With **right** side facing and working in sps and in free loops of beginning ch ***(Fig. 2, page 69)***, join Blue with slip st in first ch; slip st in next sp, (ch 1, slip st in next sp) across to ch at base of last sc, slip st in last ch; finish off.

Holding 2 strands of corresponding color yarn together, each 17" (43 cm) long, add additional fringe in each row across short edges of Afghan ***(Figs. 6a & b, page 69)***.

Baby's Best Blankie

Finished Size: 37 1/2" x 48" (95.5 cm x 122 cm)

MATERIALS

Sport Weight Yarn:
White - 14 ounces, 1,275 yards (400 grams, 1,166 meters)
Green - 7 1/2 ounces, 685 yards (210 grams, 626.5 meters)
Pink - 7 1/4 ounces, 660 yards (205 grams, 603.5 meters)
Crochet hooks, sizes F (3.75 mm) **and** G (4 mm) **or** sizes needed for gauge

GAUGE: With larger size hook, in pattern,
4 repeats = 4 1/2" (11.5 cm);
16 rows = 4 3/4" (12 cm)

Gauge Swatch: 4 1/4"w x 4 3/4"h (10.75 cm x 12 cm)
With larger size hook and White, ch 16.
Work same as Afghan Body for 16 rows.

Each row is worked across length of Afghan. When joining yarn and finishing off, leave a 6" (15 cm) end to be worked into fringe.

STITCH GUIDE

TREBLE CROCHET *(abbreviated tr)*
YO twice, insert hook in st indicated, YO and pull up a loop (4 loops on hook), (YO and draw through 2 loops on hook) 3 times.

AFGHAN BODY

With larger size hook and White, ch 172.

Row 1 (Wrong side): Sc in second ch from hook and in each ch across; finish off: 171 sc.

Note: Loop a short piece of yarn around **back** of any stitch on Row 1 to mark **right** side.

Row 2: With **right** side facing, join Green with sc in first sc ***(see Joining With Sc, page 68)***; ch 1, skip next st, sc in next sc, ★ ch 3, skip next st, sc in next sc, ch 1, skip next st, sc in next sc; repeat from ★ across; finish off: 86 sc, 43 ch-1 sps, and 42 ch-3 sps.

Row 3: With **wrong** side facing, join White with sc in first sc; working **behind** next ch-1 ***(Fig. 4, page 69)***, dc in skipped st one row **below**, ★ ch 1, working in **front** of next ch-3, dc in skipped st one row **below**, ch 1, working **behind** next ch-1, dc in skipped st one row **below**; repeat from ★ across to last sc on previous row, sc in last sc; finish off: 87 sts and 84 ch-1 sps.

Row 4: With **right** side facing, join Green with dc in first sc ***(see Joining With Dc, page 68)***; ch 1, ★ skip next dc, working **behind** next ch-1, tr in skipped sc one row **below**, ch 2, working in **front** of next dc, slip st in next ch-3 sp one row **below**, ch 2, working **behind** next ch-1, tr in skipped sc one row **below**, ch 1, repeat from ★ across to last 2 sts, skip next dc, dc in last sc; finish off: 84 tr, 2 dc, and 127 sps.

Row 5: With **wrong** side facing, join White with sc in first dc; working **behind** next ch-1, tr in skipped dc one row **below**, ★ sc in next tr on previous row, working in **front** of next 2 ch-2 sps, tr in skipped dc one row **below**, sc in next tr on previous row, working **behind** next ch-1, tr in skipped dc one row **below**; repeat from ★ across to last dc on previous row, sc in last dc; finish off: 171 sts.

Row 6: With Pink, repeat Row 2.

Row 7: Repeat Row 3.

Row 8: With Pink, repeat Row 4.

Row 9: Repeat Row 5.

Rows 10-125: Repeat Rows 2-9, 14 times; then repeat Rows 2-5 once **more**.

TRIM

FIRST SIDE

With **right** side facing and smaller size hook, join White with slip st in first sc on Row 125; (ch 2, skip next tr, slip st in next sc) across; finish off.

SECOND SIDE

With **right** side facing, using smaller size hook, and working in free loops of beginning ch ***(Fig. 2, page 69)***, join White with slip st in ch at base of first sc; (ch 2, skip next ch, slip st in next ch) across; finish off.

Holding 2 strands of corresponding color yarn together, each 13" (33 cm) long, add additional fringe in each row across short edges of Afghan ***(Figs. 6a & b, page 69)***.

Clown Carnival

Finished Size: 43" x 60" (109 cm x 152.5 cm)

MATERIALS

Worsted Weight Yarn:
- Blue - 21 ounces, 1,270 yards (600 grams, 1,161.5 meters)
- White - 18½ ounces, 1,120 yards (530 grams, 1,024 meters)
- Red - 6½ ounces, 395 yards (180 grams, 361 meters)
- Yellow - 4½ ounces, 270 yards (130 grams, 247 meters)
- Orange - 3½ ounces, 210 yards (100 grams, 192 meters)
- Green - 3½ ounces, 210 yards (100 grams, 192 meters)
- Black - ½ ounce, 30 yards (20 grams, 27.5 meters)

Crochet hook, size I (5.5 mm) **or** size needed for gauge

Yarn needle

GAUGE: Each Motif = 4½" (11.5 cm) from straight edge to straight edge

Gauge Swatch: 2" (5 cm) diameter
Work same as Circle Motif through Rnd 3.

STITCH GUIDE

DECREASE (uses next 2 dc)
YO, † insert hook in **next** dc, YO and pull up a loop, YO and draw through 2 loops on hook †, YO, skip next joining, repeat from † to † once, YO and draw through all 3 loops on hook.

CIRCLE MOTIF (Make 88)

Working Rnds 1-4 with Orange, Green, Yellow, or Red, make 22 Circle Motifs with **each** color.

Rnd 1 (Right side)**:** Ch 2, 6 sc in second ch from hook; join with slip st to first sc.

Note: Loop a short piece of yarn around any stitch to mark Rnd 1 as **right** side.

Rnd 2: Ch 1, 2 sc in same st and in each sc around; join with slip st to first sc: 12 sc.

Rnd 3: Ch 1, 2 sc in same st, sc in next sc, (2 sc in next sc, sc in next sc) around; join with slip st to first sc: 18 sc.

Rnd 4: Ch 1, 2 sc in same st, sc in next 2 sc, (2 sc in next sc, sc in next 2 sc) around; join with slip st to first sc, finish off: 24 sc.

Rnd 5: With **right** side facing, join White with sc in same st as joining ***(see Joining With Sc, page 68)***; sc in same st and in next 3 sc, (2 sc in next sc, sc in next 3 sc) around; join with slip st to first sc: 30 sc.

Rnd 6: Ch 1, 2 sc in same st, sc in next 4 sc, (2 sc in next sc, sc in next 4 sc) around; join with slip st to first sc, finish off: 36 sc.

Rnd 7: With **right** side facing, join Blue with sc in same st as joining; hdc in next sc, (dc, ch 1, dc) in next sc, hdc in next sc, ★ sc in next 3 sc, hdc in next sc, (dc, ch 1, dc) in next sc, hdc in next sc; repeat from ★ around to last 2 sc, sc in last 2 sc; join with slip st to first sc, finish off: 42 sts and 6 ch-1 sps.

CLOWN MOTIF (Make 40)

Rnds 1-4: With White, work same as Circle Motif; at end of Rnd 4, do **not** finish off: 24 sc.

Rnd 5: Ch 1, 2 sc in same st, sc in next 3 sc, (2 sc in next sc, sc in next 3 sc) around; join with slip st to first sc: 30 sc.

Rnd 6: Ch 1, sc in same st and in next 2 sc, place marker around last 2 sc made for Bow Tie placement, sc in next 2 sc, (2 sc in next sc, sc in next 4 sc) around, sc in same st as first sc; join with slip st to first sc, finish off: 36 sc.

Rnd 7: With **right** side facing, join Blue with sc in same st as joining; hdc in next sc, (dc, ch 1, dc) in next sc, hdc in next sc, ★ sc in next 3 sc, hdc in next sc, (dc, ch 1, dc) in next sc, hdc in next sc; repeat from ★ around to last 2 sc, sc in last 2 sc; join with slip st to first sc, finish off: 42 sts and 6 ch-1 sps.

Continued on page 12.

BOW TIE

Use Orange and Green for 13 Clown Motifs **each** and Red for 14 Clown Motifs.

Ch 11, dc in fourth ch from hook, † hdc in next ch, sc in next ch, slip st in next 2 chs, sc in next ch, hdc in next ch †, (dc, ch 3, slip st, ch 3, dc) in last ch; working in free loops of beginning ch ***(Fig. 2, page 69)***, repeat from † to † once, (dc, ch 3, slip st) in next ch; finish off.

CENTER

Leaving a 6" (15 cm) length for sewing, ch 4; finish off leaving a 6" (15 cm) length.

Tie Center around middle of Bow Tie having chains at front. Sew Center of Bow Tie to marked sc on Rnd 6 of Clown Motif.

NOSE

Cut a piece of cardboard 1 1/4" (3 cm) square. With Red, wrap yarn 20 times around the cardboard. Carefully slip the yarn off the cardboard and firmly tie a 12" (30.5 cm) length of Red around the middle. Leaving yarn ends to attach Nose, cut the loops on both ends and trim into a smooth ball.

Using photo as a guide for placement, sew Nose to Rnd 1 on Clown Motif below center hole.

EAR (Make 2)

With Yellow and leaving a 6" (15 cm) length for sewing, ch 2, 8 sc in second ch from hook; join with slip st to first sc, finish off leaving a 6" (15 cm) length for sewing.

Using photo as a guide for placement, sew Ears to Clown Motif.

EYES

Using photo as a guide for placement and holding two strands of Black together, work two straight stitches to form a plus sign for each eye.

HALF MOTIF (Make 14)

Row 1: With Blue, ch 4, 6 dc in fourth ch from hook.

Row 2 (Right side)**:** Ch 3 **(counts as first dc, now and throughout)**, turn; dc in same st, 2 dc in next dc and in each dc across, dc in next ch: 13 dc.

Note: Mark Row 2 as **right** side.

Row 3: Ch 3, turn; dc in same st, (dc in next dc, 2 dc in next dc) 5 times, dc in last 2 dc: 19 dc.

Row 4: Ch 3, turn; dc in same st, hdc in next dc, sc in next 3 dc, hdc in next dc, ★ (dc, ch 1, dc) in next dc, hdc in next dc, sc in next 3 dc, hdc in next dc; repeat from ★ once **more**, 2 dc in last dc, finish off: 23 sts and 2 ch-1 sps.

ASSEMBLY

With Blue and using Placement Diagram as a guide, whipstitch Motifs together forming 8 horizontal strips of 9 Motifs each and 7 horizontal strips of 8 Motifs and 2 Half Motifs each ***(Fig. 5, page 69)***, beginning in first corner ch and ending in next corner ch; then whipstitch strips together beginning in first dc on Half Motif and corner ch on Motif and ending in last dc on Half Motif and last corner ch on Motif.

KEY

- Orange
- Green
- Red
- Half Motif
- Orange Clown Motif
- Green Clown Motif
- Red Clown Motif

EDGING

Rnd 1: With **right** side facing and working across short edge, join Blue with dc in first unworked ch-1 sp of first corner Motif ***(see Joining With Dc, page 68)***; † ch 1, dc in next dc, ch 1, (skip next st, dc in next st, ch 1) 3 times, [dc in next ch-1 sp, ch 1, (dc in next st, ch 1, skip next st) 3 times, decrease, ch 1, (skip next st, dc in next st, ch 1) 3 times] 8 times, [dc in next ch-1 sp, ch 1, dc in next dc, ch 1, (skip next st, dc in next st, ch 1) 3 times] twice, ★ skip next joining; working in end of rows on Half Motif, (hdc in next row, ch 1) 8 times, skip next joining; working across next Motif, dc in next dc, ch 1, (skip next st, dc in next st, ch 1) 3 times; repeat from ★ 6 times **more** †, dc in next ch-1 sp, place marker around dc just made for st placement, repeat from † to † once; join with slip st to first dc: 326 sts and 326 ch-1 sps.

PLACEMENT DIAGRAM

Rnd 2: Ch 1, sc in same st, ch 1, (sc in next ch-1 sp, ch 1) 5 times, sc in next dc, ch 1, [(sc in next ch-1 sp, ch 1) 8 times, sc in next dc, ch 1] 8 times, (sc in next ch-1 sp, ch 1) 5 times, sc in next dc, ch 1, (sc in next ch-1 sp, ch 1) across to marked dc, sc in marked dc, ch 1, (sc in next ch-1 sp, ch 1) 5 times, sc in next dc, (ch 1, sc in next ch-1 sp) 4 times, place marker around last ch-1 made for st placement, ch 1, (sc in next ch-1 sp, ch 1) 4 times, sc in next dc, ch 1, [(sc in next ch-1 sp, ch 1) 8 times, sc in next dc, ch 1] 7 times, (sc in next ch-1 sp, ch 1) 5 times, sc in next dc, ch 1, (sc in next ch-1 sp, ch 1) across; join with slip st to first sc: 348 sc and 348 ch-1 sps.

Rnd 3: (Slip st, ch 1, sc) in first ch-1 sp, ch 1, (sc in next ch-1 sp, ch 1) 8 times, † sc in next 3 ch-1 sps, ch 1, [(sc in next ch-1 sp, ch 1) 6 times, sc in next 3 ch-1 sps, ch 1] 7 times †, (sc in next ch-1 sp, ch 1) around to marked ch-1 sp, repeat from † to † once, (sc in next ch-1 sp, ch 1) around; join with slip st to first sc: 348 sc and 316 ch-1 sps.

Rnd 4: Slip st in first ch-1 sp, (ch 2, slip st in next ch-1 sp) 8 times, † ch 1, skip next sc, slip st in next sc, ch 1, slip st in next ch-1 sp, ★ (ch 2, slip st in next ch-1 sp) 6 times, ch 1, skip next sc, slip st in next sc, ch 1, slip st in next ch-1 sp; repeat from ★ 6 times **more** †, (ch 2, slip st in next ch-1 sp) around to next 3-sc group, repeat from † to † once, ch 2, (slip st in next ch-1 sp, ch 2) across; join with slip st to first slip st, finish off.

Double-Take

Finished Size: 47" x 64"
(119.5 cm x 162.5 cm)

MATERIALS

Worsted Weight Yarn:
Plum - 35 ounces, 1,980 yards
(990 grams, 1,810.5 meters)
Dk Plum - 21 ounces, 1,190 yards
(600 grams, 1,088 meters)
Lt Lavender - 13 ounces, 735 yards
(370 grams, 672 meters)
Variegated - 9 ounces, 520 yards
(260 grams, 475.5 meters)
Crochet hook, size K (6.5 mm) **or** size needed for gauge
Yarn needle

Each row is worked across length of Afghan holding two strands of yarn together. When joining yarn and finishing off, leave a 9" (23 cm) end to be worked into fringe.

GAUGE: In pattern,
(sc, ch 2) 4 times = 4" (10 cm)
Narrow Strip = 2¾"w x 64"h
(7 cm x 162.5 cm)
Wide Strip = 4½"w x 64"h
(11.5 cm x 162.5 cm)

Gauge Swatch: 2¾"w x 4½"h
(7 cm x 11.5 cm)
Holding one strand of Plum and one strand of Lt Lavender together, ch 14.
Work same as Narrow Strip.

NARROW STRIP (Make 7)

FIRST HALF

Holding one strand of Plum and one strand of Lt Lavender together, ch 191.

Row 1 (Right side)**:** Sc in second ch from hook, ★ ch 2, skip next 2 chs, sc in next ch; repeat from ★ across; finish off: 64 sc and 63 ch-2 sps.

Note: Loop a short piece of yarn around last sc made on Row 1 to mark **right** side and **bottom** edge.

Row 2: With **wrong** side facing and holding two strands of Plum together, join yarn with sc in first sc ***(see Joining With Sc, page 68)***; (ch 2, sc in next sc) across; finish off.

Row 3: With **right** side facing and holding two strands of Dk Plum together, join yarn with sc in first sc; (ch 2, sc in next sc) across; finish off.

SECOND HALF

Row 1: With **right** side facing, working in free loops of beginning ch ***(Fig. 2, page 69)***, and holding one strand of Plum and one strand of Lavender together, join yarn with sc in first ch; ★ ch 2, skip next 2 chs, sc in next ch; repeat from ★ across; finish off: 64 sc and 63 ch-2 sps.

Rows 2 and 3: Work same as First Half.

WIDE STRIP (Make 6)

FIRST HALF

Holding one strand of Plum and one strand of Lt Lavender together, ch 191.

Row 1 (Right side)**:** Sc in second ch from hook, ★ ch 2, skip next 2 chs, sc in next ch; repeat from ★ across; finish off: 64 sc and 63 ch-2 sps.

Note: Mark last sc made on Row 1 as **right** side and **bottom** edge.

Row 2: With **wrong** side facing and holding two strands of Plum together, join yarn with sc in first sc; (ch 2, sc in next sc) across; finish off.

Row 3: With **right** side facing and holding one strand of Variegated and one strand of Plum together, join yarn with sc in first sc; (ch 2, sc in next sc) across; finish off.

Row 4: With **wrong** side facing and holding one strand of Variegated and one strand of Plum together, join yarn with sc in first sc; (ch 2, sc in next sc) across; finish off.

Row 5: With **right** side facing and holding two strands of Dk Plum together, join yarn with sc in first sc; (ch 2, sc in next sc) across; finish off.

SECOND HALF

Row 1: With **right** side facing, working in free loops of beginning ch, and holding one strand of Plum and one strand of Lt Lavender together, join yarn with sc in first ch; (ch 2, skip next 2 chs, sc in next ch) across; finish off: 64 sc and 63 ch-2 sps.

Rows 2-5: Work same as First Half.

ASSEMBLY

Holding Narrow and Wide Strips together, with bottom edges at the same end and using one strand of Dk Plum, whipstitch Strips together ***(Fig. 5, page 69)***, beginning in first sc and ending in last sc. Join remaining Strips in same manner, alternating Narrow and Wide Strips.

TRIM

FIRST SIDE

Row 1: With **wrong** side of long edge facing and holding two strands of Dk Plum together, join yarn with sc in first sc; (ch 2, sc in next sc) across; finish off.

Row 2: With **right** side facing and holding two strands of Dk Plum together, join yarn with slip st in first sc; (ch 2, slip st in next sc) across; finish off.

SECOND SIDE

Work same as First Side.

Holding 8 strands of corresponding color yarns together, each 19" (48.5 cm) long, add additional fringe across short edges of Afghan ***(Figs. 6a & b, page 69)***.

Enchanted Lace

Finished Size: 49" x 66$^{1}/_{2}$"
(124.5 cm x 169 cm)

MATERIALS

Worsted Weight Yarn:
40 ounces, 2,175 yards
(1,140 grams, 1,989 meters)
Crochet hook, size I (5.5 mm) **or** size needed for gauge

GAUGE: In pattern, 4 3-dc groups and 8 rows = 4$^{1}/_{2}$" (11.5 cm)

Gauge Swatch: 4$^{1}/_{2}$" (11.5 cm) square

Ch 19.

Row 1 (Right side)**:** 3 Dc in fifth ch from hook **(4 skipped chs count as first dc plus one skipped ch)**, ★ ch 1, skip next 3 chs, 3 dc in next ch; repeat from ★ 2 times **more**, skip next ch, dc in last ch: 4 3-dc groups and 3 ch-1 sps.

Row 2: Ch 3 **(counts as first dc, now and throughout)**, turn; dc in next dc, ch 1, (3 dc in next ch-1 sp, ch 1) 3 times, skip next 2 dc, dc in last 2 dc: 3 3-dc groups and 4 ch-1 sps.

Row 3: Ch 3, turn; 3 dc in next ch-1 sp, (ch 1, 3 dc in next ch-1 sp) 3 times, skip next dc, dc in last dc.

Rows 4-7: Repeat Rows 2 and 3 twice.

Finish off.

AFGHAN BODY

Ch 167, place marker in third ch from hook for st placement.

Row 1 (Right side)**:** 3 Dc in fifth ch from hook **(4 skipped chs count as first dc plus one skipped ch)**, ★ ch 1, skip next 3 chs, 3 dc in next ch; repeat from ★ across to last 2 chs, skip next ch, dc in last ch: 41 3-dc groups and 40 ch-1 sps.

Note: Loop a short piece of yarn around any stitch to mark Row 1 as **right** side.

Row 2: Ch 3 **(counts as first dc, now and throughout)**, turn; dc in next dc, (ch 1, 3 dc in next ch-1 sp) twice, ch 7, ★ 3 dc in next ch-1 sp, (ch 1, 3 dc in next ch-1 sp) 3 times, ch 7; repeat from ★ across to last 2 ch-1 sps, (3 dc in next ch-1 sp, ch 1) twice, skip next 2 dc, dc in last 2 dc: 31 ch-1 sps and 10 ch-7 sps.

When instructed to work into a chain, work into top 2 loops of the chain ***(Fig. 3, page 69)***.

Row 3: Ch 3, turn; 3 dc in next ch-1 sp, ch 1, 3 dc in next ch-1 sp, ch 4, sc in center ch of next ch-7, ch 4, 3 dc in next ch-1 sp, ★ (ch 1, 3 dc in next ch-1 sp) twice, ch 4, sc in center ch of next ch-7, ch 4, 3 dc in next ch-1 sp; repeat from ★ across to last ch-1 sp, ch 1, 3 dc in last ch-1 sp, skip next dc, dc in last dc: 10 sc, 20 ch-1 sps, and 20 ch-4 sps.

Row 4: Ch 3, turn; dc in next dc, ch 1, ★ 3 dc in next ch-1 sp, ch 4, sc in next ch-4 sp, sc in next sc and in next ch-4 sp, ch 4, 3 dc in next ch-1 sp, ch 1; repeat from ★ across to last 4 dc, skip next 2 dc, dc in last 2 dc: 30 sc, 11 ch-1 sps, and 20 ch-4 sps.

Row 5: Ch 3, turn; 3 dc in next ch-1 sp,★ ch 5, sc in next ch-4 sp, sc in next 3 sc and in next ch-4 sp, ch 5, 3 dc in next ch-1 sp; repeat from ★ across to last 2 dc, skip next dc, dc in last dc: 50 sc and 20 ch-5 sps.

Row 6: Ch 3, turn; dc in next dc, ch 1, skip next 2 dc, ★ 3 dc in first ch of next ch-5, ch 5, skip next sc, sc in next 3 sc, ch 5, 3 dc in fifth ch of next ch-5, ch 1; repeat from ★ across to last 4 dc, skip next 2 dc, dc in last 2 dc: 30 sc, 11 ch-1 sps, and 20 ch-5 sps.

Row 7: Ch 3, turn; 3 dc in next ch-1 sp, ★ ch 1, 3 dc in first ch of next ch-5, ch 5, skip next sc, sc in next sc, ch 5, 3 dc in fifth ch of next ch-5, ch 1, 3 dc in next ch-1 sp; repeat from ★ across to last 2 dc, skip next dc, dc in last dc: 20 ch-1 sps and 20 ch-5 sps.

Row 8: Ch 3, turn; dc in next dc, ch 1, 3 dc in next ch-1 sp, ch 1, 3 dc in first ch of next ch-5, ch 1, 3 dc in fifth ch of next ch-5, ch 1, ★ (3 dc in next ch-1 sp, ch 1) twice, 3 dc in first ch of next ch-5, ch 1, 3 dc in fifth ch of next ch-5, ch 1; repeat from ★ across to last ch-1 sp, 3 dc in last ch-1 sp, ch 1, skip next 2 dc, dc in last 2 dc: 41 ch-1 sps.

Row 9: Ch 3, turn; 3 dc in next ch-1 sp, (ch 1, 3 dc in next ch-1 sp) across to last 2 dc, skip next dc, dc in last dc: 40 ch-1 sps.

Rows 10-113: Repeat Rows 2-9, 13 times; at end of Row 113, do **not** finish off: 125 dc and 40 ch-1 sps.

EDGING

Rnd 1: Ch 1, do **not** turn; (sc, ch 2, sc) in top of last dc made, ch 1; working around dc at end of rows, skip Row 113, (sc in next row, ch 1) across to Row 1, skip Row 1; working in free loops of beginning ch ***(Fig. 2, page 69)*** and in 2 loops of unworked chs, (sc, ch 2, sc) in first ch, ch 1, skip next ch, (sc in next ch, ch 1, skip next ch) across to marked ch, (sc, ch 2, sc) in marked ch, ch 1; working around dc at end of rows, skip Row 1, (sc in next row, ch 1) across to last row, skip last row; working across Row 113, (sc, ch 2, sc) in first dc, ch 1, skip next dc, sc in next dc, ch 1, ★ sc in next ch-1 sp, ch 1, skip next dc, sc in next dc, ch 1; repeat from ★ across; join with slip st to first sc: 392 sps.

Rnd 2: Slip st in next corner ch-2 sp, ch 1, ★ (sc, ch 3, sc) in corner ch-2 sp, ch 1, (sc in next ch-1 sp, ch 1) across to next corner ch-2 sp; repeat from ★ around; join with slip st to first sc: 396 sps.

Rnd 3: Slip st in next corner ch-3 sp, ch 3, (2 dc, ch 3, 3 dc) in same sp, ch 1, skip next ch-1 sp, (3 dc in next ch-1 sp, ch 1, skip next ch-1 sp) across to next corner ch-3 sp, ★ (3 dc, ch 3, 3 dc) in corner ch-3 sp, ch 1, (skip next ch-1 sp, 3 dc in next ch-1 sp, ch 1) across to next corner ch-3 sp; repeat from ★ 2 times **more**; join with slip st to first dc: 202 3-dc groups and 202 sps.

Rnd 4: Slip st in next dc, ch 6, dc in same st, (sc, dc, ch 2, dc, sc) in next corner ch-3 sp, ★ skip next dc, (dc, ch 2, dc) in next dc, **[**sc in next ch-1 sp, skip next dc, (dc, ch 2, dc) in next dc**]** across to next corner ch-3 sp, (sc, dc, ch 2, dc, sc) in corner ch-3 sp; repeat from ★ 2 times **more**, **[**skip next dc, (dc, ch 2, dc) in next dc, sc in next ch-1 sp**]** across; join with slip st to third ch of beginning ch-6, finish off.

Flowers for Thought

Finished Size: 48" x $67^1/_2$"
(122 cm x 171.5 cm)

MATERIALS

Worsted Weight Yarn:
- Ecru - 36 ounces, 2,470 yards (1,020 grams, 2,258.5 meters)
- Green - 9 ounces, 615 yards (260 grams, 562.5 meters)
- Blue - $2^1/_2$ ounces, 170 yards (70 grams, 155.5 meters)
- Rose - $2^1/_2$ ounces, 170 yards (70 grams, 155.5 meters)
- Gold - $2^1/_2$ ounces, 170 yards (70 grams, 155.5 meters)

Crochet hook, size I (5.5 mm) **or** size needed for gauge

Yarn needle

GAUGE: Each Square = $6^1/_2$" (16.5 cm)

Gauge Swatch: $3^3/_4$" (9.5 cm) diameter
Work same as Square A through Rnd 4.

STITCH GUIDE

TREBLE CROCHET *(abbreviated tr)*
YO twice, insert hook in sp indicated, YO and pull up a loop (4 loops on hook), (YO and draw through 2 loops on hook) 3 times.

CLUSTER
Ch 3, YO, insert hook in third ch from hook, YO and pull up a loop, YO and draw through 2 loops on hook, YO, insert hook in same ch, YO and pull up a loop, YO and draw through 2 loops on hook, YO and draw through all 3 loops on hook.

SQUARE A (Make 35)

Rnd 1 (Right side)**:** With Gold, ch 5, (dc, ch 1) 7 times in fifth ch from hook; join with slip st to fourth ch of beginning ch-5, finish off: 8 sts and 8 ch-1 sps.

Note: Loop a short piece of yarn around any stitch to mark Rnd 1 as **right** side.

Rnd 2: With **wrong** side facing, join Rose with slip st in same st as joining; work Cluster, (slip st in next dc, work Cluster) around; join with slip st to first slip st, finish off: 8 Clusters.

Rnd 3: With **right** side facing, working **behind** Clusters ***(Fig. 4, page 69)*** and in ch-1 sps on Rnd 1, join Green with sc in any ch-1 sp ***(see Joining With Sc, page 68)***; ch 3, (sc in next ch-1 sp, ch 3) around; join with slip st to first sc: 8 ch-3 sps.

Rnd 4: Ch 1, **[**sc, ch 1, (dc, ch 1) twice, sc**]** in next ch-3 sp (Leaf made) and in each ch-3 sp around; join with slip st to first sc, finish off: 8 Leaves.

Rnd 5: With **right** side facing, join Ecru with dc in center ch-1 sp of any Leaf ***(see Joining With Dc, page 68)***; ch 3, dc in same sp, ★ ch 2, (dc, ch 3, dc) in center ch-1 sp of next Leaf; repeat from ★ around, ch 1, sc in first dc to form last ch-2 sp: 16 sps.

Rnd 6: Ch 6 **(counts as first tr plus ch 2)**, (hdc in next sp, ch 2) 3 times, ★ (tr, ch 5, tr) in next ch-2 sp, ch 2, (hdc in next sp, ch 2) 3 times; repeat from ★ 2 times **more**, tr in same sp as first tr, ch 2, dc in first tr to form last ch-5 sp: 20 sps.

Rnd 7: Ch 3 **(counts as first dc)**, 2 dc in last ch-5 sp made, dc in next tr, (2 dc in next ch-2 sp, dc in next st) 4 times, ★ (3 dc, ch 3, 3 dc) in next corner ch-5 sp, dc in next tr, (2 dc in next ch-2 sp, dc in next st) 4 times; repeat from ★ 2 times **more**, 3 dc in same sp as first dc, ch 3; join with slip st to first dc, finish off: 76 dc and 4 ch-3 sps.

SQUARE B (Make 35)

Rnd 1 (Right side)**:** With Gold, ch 5, (dc, ch 1) 7 times in fifth ch from hook; join with slip st to fourth ch of beginning ch-5, finish off: 8 sts and 8 ch-1 sps.

Note: Mark Rnd 1 as **right** side.

Rnd 2: With **wrong** side facing, join Blue with slip st in same st as joining; work Cluster, (slip st in next dc, work Cluster) around; join with slip st to first slip st, finish off: 8 Clusters.

Rnds 3-7: Work same as Square A: 76 dc and 4 ch-3 sps.

ASSEMBLY

With Ecru and using Placement Diagram as a guide, whipstitch Squares together forming 7 vertical strips of 10 Squares each ***(Fig. 5, page 69)***, beginning in center ch of first corner ch-3 and ending in center ch of next corner ch-3; then whipstitch strips together in same manner.

PLACEMENT DIAGRAM

A	B	A	B	A	B	A
B	A	B	A	B	A	B
A	B	A	B	A	B	A
B	A	B	A	B	A	B
A	B	A	B	A	B	A
B	A	B	A	B	A	B
A	B	A	B	A	B	A
B	A	B	A	B	A	B
A	B	A	B	A	B	A
B	A	B	A	B	A	B

EDGING

Rnd 1: With **right** side facing, join Ecru with sc in any corner ch-3 sp; ch 2, sc in same sp, ★ † ch 1, skip next dc, (sc in next dc, ch 1, skip next dc) 9 times, **[**(hdc in next sp, ch 1) twice, skip next dc, (sc in next dc, ch 1, skip next dc) 9 times**]** across to next corner ch-3 sp †, (sc, ch 2, sc) in corner ch-3 sp; repeat from ★ 2 times **more**, then repeat from † to † once; join with slip st to first sc: 374 sps.

Rnd 2: Slip st in next corner ch-2 sp, ch 1, ★ (sc, ch 2, sc) in corner ch-2 sp, ch 1, (sc in next ch-1 sp, ch 1) across to next corner ch-2 sp; repeat from ★ around; join with slip st to first sc: 378 sps.

Rnd 3: Slip st in corner ch-2 sp, ch 6, dc in same sp, ch 1, (dc in next ch-1 sp, ch 1) across to next corner ch-2 sp, ★ (dc, ch 3, dc) in corner ch-2 sp, ch 1, (dc in next ch-1 sp, ch 1) across to next corner ch-2 sp; repeat from ★ 2 times **more**; join with slip st to third ch of beginning ch-6: 382 sps.

Rnd 4: ★ (Slip st, ch 3, slip st) in corner ch-3 sp, ch 2, (slip st in next ch-1 sp, ch 2) across to next corner ch-3 sp; repeat from ★ around; join with slip st to first slip st, finish off.

Glimpse of Granny

Finished Size: 47" x 68"
(119.5 cm x 172.5 cm)

MATERIALS

Worsted Weight Yarn:
- White - 24 ounces, 1,575 yards (680 grams, 1,440 meters)
- Green - 7 ounces, 460 yards (200 grams, 420.5 meters)
- Purple - $5^1/_2$ ounces, 360 yards (160 grams, 329 meters)
- Teal - 3 ounces, 195 yards, (90 grams, 178.5 meters)

Crochet hook, size I (5.5 mm) **or** size needed for gauge

Yarn needle

GAUGE: Each Square = $5^1/_4$" (13.25 cm)

Gauge Swatch: 3" (7.5 cm) square
Work same as Square A through Rnd 2.

SQUARE A (Make 39)

Rnd 1 (Right side)**:** With Teal, ch 4, 2 dc in fourth ch from hook, ch 3, (3 dc in same ch, ch 3) 3 times; join with slip st to top of beginning ch-4, finish off: 12 dc and 4 ch-3 sps.

Note: Loop a short piece of yarn around any stitch to mark Rnd 1 as **right** side.

Rnd 2: With **right** side facing, join Purple with dc in any ch-3 sp ***(see Joining With Dc, page 68)***; (2 dc, ch 3, 3 dc) in same sp, ch 1, ★ (3 dc, ch 3, 3 dc) in next ch-3 sp, ch 1; repeat from ★ 2 times **more**; join with slip st to first dc, finish off: 24 dc and 8 sps.

Rnd 3: With **right** side facing, join Green with dc in any corner ch-3 sp; (2 dc, ch 3, 3 dc) in same sp, ch 1, 3 dc in next ch-1 sp, ch 1, ★ (3 dc, ch 3, 3 dc) in next corner ch-3 sp, ch 1, 3 dc in next ch-1 sp, ch 1; repeat from ★ 2 times **more**; join with slip st to first dc, finish off: 36 dc and 12 sps.

Rnd 4: With **right** side facing, join White with dc in any corner ch-3 sp; (2 dc, ch 3, 3 dc) in same sp, ch 1, (3 dc in next ch-1 sp, ch 1) twice, ★ (3 dc, ch 3, 3 dc) in next corner ch-3 sp, ch 1, (3 dc in next ch-1 sp, ch 1) twice; repeat from ★ 2 times **more**; join with slip st to first dc, finish off: 48 dc and 16 sps.

SQUARE B (Make 38)

Rnd 1 (Right side)**:** With White, ch 4, 2 dc in fourth ch from hook, (ch 3, 3 dc in same ch) 3 times, dc in first dc to form last ch-3 sp: 12 dc and 4 ch-3 sps.

Note: Mark Rnd 1 as **right** side.

Rnd 2: Ch 1, (sc, ch 7, sc) in last ch-3 sp made, ★ ch 5, (sc, ch 7, sc) in next corner ch-3 sp; repeat from ★ 2 times **more**, ch 2, dc in first sc to form last ch-5 sp: 8 sps.

Rnd 3: Ch 3 **(counts as first dc, now and throughout)**, 2 dc in last ch-5 sp made, ch 1, (3 dc, ch 3, 3 dc) in next corner ch-7 sp, ★ ch 1, 3 dc in next ch-5 sp, ch 1, (3 dc, ch 3, 3 dc) in next corner ch-7 sp; repeat from ★ 2 times **more**, sc in first dc to form last ch-1 sp: 36 dc and 12 sps.

Rnd 4: Ch 3, 2 dc in last ch-1 sp made, ch 1, 3 dc in next ch-1 sp, ch 1, (3 dc, ch 3, 3 dc) in next corner ch-3 sp, ch 1, ★ (3 dc in next ch-1 sp, ch 1) twice, (3 dc, ch 3, 3 dc) in next corner ch-3 sp, ch 1; repeat from ★ 2 times **more**; join with slip st to first dc, finish off: 48 dc and 16 sps.

ASSEMBLY

With White and using Placement Diagram as a guide, whipstitch Squares together forming 7 vertical strips of 11 Squares each ***(Fig. 5, page 69)***, beginning in center ch of first corner ch-3 and ending in center ch of next corner ch-3; then whipstitch strips together in same manner.

PLACEMENT DIAGRAM

A	B	A	B	A	B	A
B	A	B	A	B	A	B
A	B	A	B	A	B	A
B	A	B	A	B	A	B
A	B	A	B	A	B	A
B	A	B	A	B	A	B
A	B	A	B	A	B	A
B	A	B	A	B	A	B
A	B	A	B	A	B	A
B	A	B	A	B	A	B
A	B	A	B	A	B	A

EDGING

Rnd 1: With **right** side facing, join White with sc in any corner ch-3 sp ***(see Joining With Sc, page 68)***; ch 3, sc in same sp, ★ † ch 1, skip next dc, sc in next dc, ch 1, (sc in next ch-1 sp, ch 1, skip next dc, sc in next dc, ch 1) 3 times, [(sc in next sp, ch 1) twice, skip next dc, sc in next dc, ch 1, (sc in next ch-1 sp, ch 1, skip next dc, sc in next dc, ch 1) 3 times] across to next corner ch-3 sp †, (sc, ch 3, sc) in corner ch-3 sp; repeat from ★ 2 times **more**, then repeat from † to † once; join with slip st to first sc: 324 sps.

Rnd 2: Slip st in corner ch-3 sp, ch 1, ★ (sc, ch 3, sc) in corner ch-3 sp, ch 1, (sc in next ch-1 sp, ch 1) across to next corner ch-3 sp; repeat from ★ around; join with slip st to first sc: 328 sps.

Rnd 3: (Slip st, ch 3, 2 dc, ch 3, 3 dc) in first corner ch-3 sp, ★ † ch 1, skip next ch-1 sp, (3 dc in next ch-1 sp, ch 1, skip next ch-1 sp) across to next corner ch-3 sp †, (3 dc, ch 3, 3 dc) in corner ch-3 sp; repeat from ★ 2 times **more**, then repeat from † to † once; join with slip st to first dc, finish off: 168 sps.

Rnd 4: With **right** side facing, join Green with dc in any corner ch-3 sp; (2 dc, ch 3, 3 dc) in same sp, ch 1, (3 dc in next ch-1 sp, ch 1) across to next corner ch-3 sp, ★ (3 dc, ch 3, 3 dc) in corner ch-3 sp, ch 1, (3 dc in next ch-1 sp, ch 1) across to next corner ch-3 sp; repeat from ★ 2 times **more**; join with slip st to first dc, finish off: 172 sps.

Rnd 5: With Purple, repeat Rnd 4: 176 sps.

Rnd 6: With Teal, repeat Rnd 4: 180 sps.

Rnd 7: With Purple, repeat Rnd 4: 184 sps.

Rnd 8: Repeat Rnd 4: 188 sps.

Rnd 9: With **right** side facing, join White with dc in any corner ch-3 sp; 2 dc in same sp, ch 1, (3 dc in next ch-1 sp, ch 1) across to next corner ch-3 sp, ★ (3 dc, ch 3, 3 dc) in corner ch-3 sp, ch 1, (3 dc in next ch-1 sp, ch 1) across to next corner ch-3 sp; repeat from ★ 2 times **more**, 3 dc in same sp as first dc, dc in first dc to form last corner ch-3 sp: 192 sps.

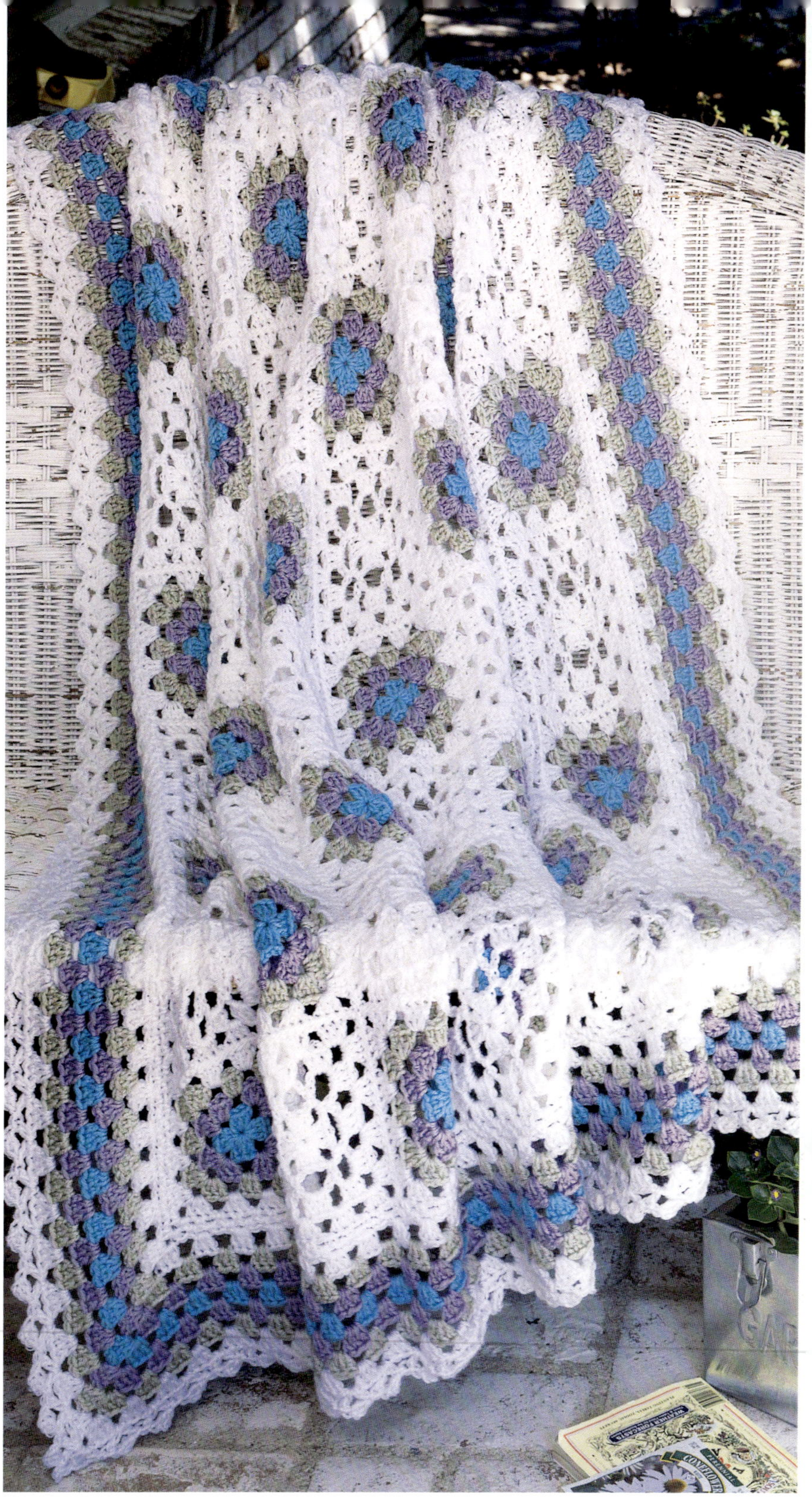

Rnd 10: Ch 6, dc in third ch from hook, dc in same sp, (ch 3, dc in third ch from hook, dc in same sp) twice, ★ † [dc in next ch-1 sp, (ch 3, dc in third ch from hook, dc in same sp)] across to next corner ch-3 sp †, dc in corner ch-3 sp, (ch 3, dc in third ch from hook, dc in same sp) 3 times; repeat from ★ 2 times **more**, then repeat from † to † once; join with slip st to third ch of beginning ch-6, finish off.

Handmade Hearts

Finished Size: 48" x 65" (122 cm x 165 cm)

MATERIALS

Worsted Weight Yarn:
Ecru - 39 ounces, 2,560 yards (1,110 grams, 2,341 meters)
Rose - $3^1/_2$ ounces, 230 yards (100 grams, 210.5 meters)
Green - $3^1/_2$ ounces, 230 yards (100 grams, 210.5 meters)
Crochet hook, size I (5.5 mm) **or** size needed for gauge
Yarn needle

GAUGE: Each Square = $8^3/_4$" (22.25 cm)

Gauge Swatch: $4^1/_4$" (10.75 cm) square
Work same as Square A through Row 17.

STITCH GUIDE

CLUSTER (uses one st)
★ YO, insert hook in Back Loop Only of sc indicated ***(Fig. 1, page 68)***, YO and pull up a loop, YO and draw through 2 loops on hook; repeat from ★ 3 times **more**, YO and draw through all 5 loops on hook. Push Cluster to **right** side.

SQUARE A (Make 17)

With Ecru, ch 16.

Row 1: Sc in second ch from hook and in each ch across: 15 sc.

Row 2 (Right side)**:** Ch 1, turn; sc in each sc across.

Note: Loop a short piece of yarn around any stitch to mark Row 2 as **right** side and **bottom** edge.

Work sc in both loops of each stitch unless otherwise indicated.

Row 3: Ch 1, turn; sc in first 7 sc, work Cluster in next sc, sc in last 7 sc: 14 sc and one Cluster.

Row 4: Ch 1, turn; sc in each st across: 15 sc.

Row 5: Ch 1, turn; sc in first 5 sc, work Cluster in next sc, sc in next 3 sc, work Cluster in next sc, sc in last 5 sc: 13 sc and 2 Clusters.

Row 6: Ch 1, turn; sc in each st across: 15 sc.

Row 7: Ch 1, turn; sc in first 3 sc, work Cluster in next sc, sc in next 7 sc, work Cluster in next sc, sc in last 3 sc: 13 sc and 2 Clusters.

Row 8: Ch 1, turn; sc in each st across: 15 sc.

Row 9: Ch 1, turn; sc in first sc, work Cluster in next sc, sc in next 11 sc, work Cluster in next sc, sc in last sc: 13 sc and 2 Clusters.

Row 10: Ch 1, turn; sc in each st across: 15 sc.

Rows 11 and 12: Repeat Rows 9 and 10.

Row 13: Ch 1, turn; sc in first sc, work Cluster in next sc, (sc in next 5 sc, work Cluster in next sc) twice, sc in last sc: 12 sc and 3 Clusters.

Row 14: Ch 1, turn; sc in each st across: 15 sc.

Row 15: Ch 1, turn; sc in first 3 sc, ★ work Cluster in next sc, sc in next sc, work Cluster in next sc, sc in next 3 sc; repeat from ★ once **more**: 11 sc and 4 Clusters.

Rows 16 and 17: Ch 1, turn; sc in each st across; at end of Row 17, do **not** finish off: 15 sc.

BORDER

Rnd 1: Ch 1, turn; sc in each sc across, † ch 3, work 15 sc evenly spaced across end of rows, ch 3 †, working in free loops of beginning ch ***(Fig. 2, page 69)***, sc in ch at base of first sc and in each ch across, repeat from † to † once; join with slip st to first sc: 60 sc and 4 ch-3 sps.

Rnd 2: Ch 4, ★ † skip next sc, (dc in next 3 sc, ch 1, skip next sc) 3 times, dc in next sc, (2 dc, ch 3, 2 dc) in next corner ch-3 sp †, dc in next sc, ch 1; repeat from ★ 2 times **more**, then repeat from † to † once; join with slip st to third ch of beginning ch-4, finish off: 60 sts and 20 sps.

Rnd 3: With **right** side facing, join Rose with dc in any corner ch-3 sp ***(see Joining With Dc, page 68)***; (2 dc, ch 3, 3 dc) in same sp, ★ † ch 1, skip next 3 dc, (3 dc in next ch-1 sp, ch 1, skip next 3 dc) across to next corner ch-3 sp †, (3 dc, ch 3, 3 dc) in corner ch-3 sp; repeat from ★ 2 times **more**, then repeat from † to † once; join with slip st to first dc, finish off: 72 dc and 24 sps.

Rnd 4: With Ecru, repeat Rnd 3: 84 dc and 28 sps.

SQUARE B (Make 18)

Work same as Square A through Rnd 2 of Border: 60 sts and 20 sps.

Rnd 3: With Green, work same as Square A.

Rnd 4: Work same as Square A.

ASSEMBLY

With Ecru, using Placement Diagram as a guide, and keeping bottom edges at same end, whipstitch Squares together forming 5 vertical strips of 7 Squares each ***(Fig. 5, page 69)***, beginning in second ch of first corner ch-3 and ending in second ch of next corner ch-3; then whipstitch strips together in same manner.

PLACEMENT DIAGRAM

B	A	B	A	B
A	B	A	B	A
B	A	B	A	B
A	B	A	B	A
B	A	B	A	B
A	B	A	B	A
B	A	B	A	B

EDGING

Rnd 1: With **right** side facing, join Ecru with sc in any corner ch-3 sp ***(see Joining With Sc, page 68)***; ★ † ch 1, skip next dc, sc in next dc, ch 1, (sc in next ch-1 sp, ch 1, skip next dc, sc in next dc, ch 1) 6 times, **[**(sc in next sp, ch 1) twice, skip next dc, sc in next dc, ch 1, (sc in next ch-1 sp, ch 1, skip next dc, sc in next dc, ch 1) 6 times**]** across to next corner ch-3 sp †, (sc, ch 2, sc) in corner ch-3 sp; repeat from ★ 2 times **more**, then repeat from † to † once, sc in same sp as first sc, ch 1, sc in first sc to form last ch-2 sp: 360 sc and 360 sps.

Rnd 2: Ch 1, turn; sc in last ch-2 sp made, ★ † work Cluster in next sc, (sc in next ch-1 sp, ch 1, sc in next ch-1 sp, work Cluster in next sc) across to next corner ch-2 sp †, (sc, ch 2, sc) in corner ch-2 sp; repeat from ★ 2 times **more**, then repeat from † to † once, sc in same sp as first sc, ch 1, sc in first sc to form last ch-2 sp.

Rnd 3: Ch 1, turn; sc in last ch-2 sp made, ★ † ch 1, sc in next Cluster, ch 1, (sc in next ch-1 sp, ch 1, sc in next Cluster, ch 1) across to next corner ch-2 sp †, (sc, ch 2, sc) in corner ch-2 sp; repeat from ★ 2 times **more**, then repeat from † to † once, sc in same sp as first sc, ch 1, sc in first sc to form last ch-2 sp.

Rnds 4-7: Repeat Rnds 2 and 3 twice.

Rnd 8: Do **not** turn; slip st in last ch-2 sp made, ch 2, ★ (slip st in next ch-1 sp, ch 2) across to next corner ch-2 sp, (slip st, ch 2) twice in corner ch-2 sp; repeat from ★ 2 times **more**, (slip st in next ch-1 sp, ch 2) across, slip st in same sp as first slip st, ch 2; join with slip st to first slip st, finish off.

Incredible in White

Finished Size: 50" x 67" (127 cm x 170 cm)

MATERIALS
Worsted Weight Yarn:
47 ounces, 2,555 yards
(1,330 grams, 2,336.5 meters)
Crochet hook, size I (5.5 mm) **or** size needed for gauge
Yarn needle

GAUGE: Each Square = $5^3/_4$" (14.5 cm)

Gauge Swatch: $2^3/_4$" (7 cm) square
Work same as Square through Rnd 2.

STITCH GUIDE

TREBLE CROCHET *(abbreviated tr)*
YO twice, insert hook in st indicated, YO and pull up a loop (4 loops on hook), (YO and draw through 2 loops on hook) 3 times.

CROSS ST
Tr in next st, ch 1, working in **front** of last tr made, tr in same st as first tr of previous Cross St made.

SQUARE (Make 88)

Rnd 1 (Right side)**:** Ch 2, 8 sc in second ch from hook; join with slip st to first sc.

Note: Loop a short piece of yarn around any stitch to mark Rnd 1 as **right** side.

Rnd 2: Ch 5 **(counts as first tr plus ch 1, now and throughout)**, working in **front** of tr just made, tr in last sc on Rnd 1 **(first Cross St made)**, work 6 Cross Sts, tr in same st as second tr of first Cross St made, ch 1, working in **front** of last tr made, tr in same st as first tr made of previous Cross St; join with slip st to first tr: 8 Cross Sts.

Rnd 3: Slip st in next ch and in next tr, ch 5, working in **front** of tr just made, tr in same st as joining, work 14 Cross Sts, tr in same st as second tr of first Cross St made, ch 1, working in **front** of last tr made, tr in same st as first tr of previous Cross St made; join with slip st to first tr: 16 Cross Sts.

Rnd 4: (Slip st, ch 1, sc) in first ch-1 sp, ch 6, tr in sixth ch from hook, ch 1, sc in next ch-1 sp, ★ (ch 4, sc in next ch-1 sp) 3 times, ch 6, tr in sixth ch from hook, ch 1, sc in next ch-1 sp; repeat from ★ 2 times **more**, (ch 4, sc in next ch-1 sp) twice, ch 1, dc in first sc to form last ch-4 sp: 16 sps.

Rnd 5: Ch 4 **(counts as first hdc plus ch 2)**, (3 dc, ch 3, 3 dc) in next corner sp, ch 2, hdc in next ch-4 sp, ch 2, sc in next ch-4 sp, ch 2, ★ hdc in next ch-4 sp, ch 2, (3 dc, ch 3, 3 dc) in next corner sp, ch 2, hdc in next ch-4 sp, ch 2, sc in next ch-4 sp, ch 2; repeat from ★ 2 times **more**; join with slip st to first hdc, finish off: 36 sts and 20 sps.

ASSEMBLY

Whipstitch Squares together, forming 8 vertical strips of 11 Squares each ***(Fig. 5, page 69)***, beginning in center ch of first corner ch-3 and ending in center ch of next corner ch-3; then whipstitch strips together in same manner.

EDGING

Rnd 1: With **right** side facing, join yarn with sc in any corner ch-3 sp ***(see Joining With Sc, page 68)***; ch 3, sc in same sp, ★ † ch 1, skip next dc, sc in next dc, ch 1, sc in next ch-2 sp, ch 1, sc in next hdc, ch 1, (sc in next ch-2 sp, ch 1) twice, sc in next hdc, ch 1, sc in next ch-2 sp, ch 1, skip next dc, sc in next dc, ch 1, [(sc in next sp, ch 1) twice, skip next dc, sc in next dc, ch 1, sc in next ch-2 sp, ch 1, sc in next hdc, ch 1, (sc in next ch-2 sp, ch 1) twice, sc in next hdc, ch 1, sc in next ch-2 sp, ch 1, skip next dc, sc in next dc, ch 1] across to next corner ch-3 sp †, (sc, ch 3, sc) in corner ch-3 sp; repeat from ★ 2 times **more**, then repeat from † to † once; join with slip st to first sc: 380 sps.

Rnd 2: Slip st in next corner ch-3 sp, ch 1, ★ (sc, ch 3, sc) in corner ch-3 sp, ch 1, (sc in next ch-1 sp, ch 1) across to next corner ch-3 sp; repeat from ★ around; join with slip st to first sc: 384 sps.

Rnd 3: Ch 4 **(counts as first dc plus ch 1, now and throughout)**, ★ † (dc, ch 1) 4 times in corner ch-3 sp **(Corner Shell made)**, skip next ch-1 sp, (sc in next ch-1 sp, ch 1) 3 times, [skip

next sc, (dc, ch 1) 3 times in next sc, skip next ch-1 sp, (sc in next ch-1 sp, ch 1) 3 times] across to within 2 sc of next corner ch-3 sp, skip next sc †, dc in next sc, ch 1; repeat from ★ 2 times **more**, then repeat from † to † once; join with slip st to first dc: 236 dc and 464 ch-1 sps.

Rnd 4: Ch 4, ★ † (dc in next ch-1 sp, ch 1, dc in next dc, ch 1) 4 times, skip next ch-1 sp, (sc in next ch-1 sp, ch 1) twice, [skip next sc, dc in next dc, ch 1, (dc in next ch-1 sp, ch 1, dc in next dc, ch 1) twice, skip next ch-1 sp, (sc in next ch-1 sp, ch 1) twice] across to within one sc of next Corner Shell, skip next sc †, dc in next dc, ch 1; repeat from ★ 2 times **more**, then repeat from † to † once; join with slip st to first dc.

Rnd 5: ★ † (Ch 2, slip st in next dc) 8 times, ch 1, skip next ch-1 sp, slip st in next ch-1 sp, ch 1, [skip next sc, slip st in next dc, (ch 2, slip st in next dc) 4 times, ch 1, skip next ch-1 sp, slip st in next ch-1 sp, ch 1] across to within one sc of next Corner Shell, skip next sc †, slip st in next dc; repeat from ★ 2 times **more**, then repeat from † to † once; join with slip st to joining slip st, finish off.

Jazzy Journey

Finished Size: 45" x 57" (114.5 cm x 145 cm)

MATERIALS
Bulky Weight Yarn:
Lt Green - 23 ounces, 1,035 yards (650 grams, 946.5 meters)
Green - 20 ounces, 900 yards (570 grams, 823 meters)
Crochet hook, size K (6.5 mm) **or** size needed for gauge

GAUGE: In pattern,
one repeat (18 sts) = 6" (15 cm);
20 rows = $6^3/_4$" (17 cm)

Gauge Swatch: 9"w x $6^3/_4$"h (23 cm x 17 cm)
With Lt Green, ch 28.
Work same as Afghan Body for 20 rows.

Each row is worked across length of Afghan. When joining yarn and finishing off, leave an 8" (20.5 cm) end to be worked into fringe.

AFGHAN BODY

With Lt Green, ch 172.

Row 1 (Right side)**:** Sc in second ch from hook, ★ ch 1, skip next ch, sc in next ch; repeat from ★ across; finish off: 86 sc and 85 ch-1 sps.

Note: Loop a short piece of yarn around any stitch to mark Row 1 as **right** side.

Row 2: With **wrong** side facing, join Green with sc in first sc ***(see Joining With Sc, page 68)***; (ch 1, sc in next sc) 4 times, ★ sc in next ch-1 sp, (ch 1, sc in next ch-1 sp) 4 times, sc in next sc, (ch 1, sc in next sc) 4 times; repeat from ★ across; finish off: 95 sc and 76 ch-1 sps.

Row 3: With **right** side facing, join Lt Green with sc in first sc; (ch 1, sc in next sc) 4 times, ★ ch 1, (sc in next ch-1 sp, ch 1) 4 times, skip next sc, sc in next sc, (ch 1, sc in next sc) 4 times; repeat from ★ across; finish off: 86 sc and 85 ch-1 sps.

Row 4: With **wrong** side facing, join Green with sc in first sc; (ch 1, sc in next sc) 4 times, ★ sc in next ch-1 sp, (ch 1, sc in next ch-1 sp) 4 times, sc in next sc, (ch 1, sc in next sc) 4 times; repeat from ★ across; finish off: 95 sc and 76 ch-1 sps.

Rows 5-12: Repeat Rows 3 and 4, 4 times.

Row 13: With **right** side facing, join Lt Green with sc in first sc; sc in next ch-1 sp, (ch 1, sc in next ch-1 sp) 3 times, ★ ch 1, skip next sc, sc in next sc, (ch 1, sc in next sc) 4 times, (ch 1, sc in next ch-1 sp) 4 times; repeat from ★ across to last sc, sc in last sc; finish off: 87 sc and 84 ch-1 sps.

Row 14: With **wrong** side facing, join Green with sc in first sc; ★ (ch 1, sc in next ch-1 sp) 4 times, sc in next sc, (ch 1, sc in next sc) 4 times, sc in next ch-1 sp; repeat from ★ across to last 3 ch-1 sps, (ch 1, sc in next ch-1 sp) 3 times, ch 1, skip next sc, sc in last sc; finish off: 95 sc and 76 ch-1 sps.

Rows 15-22: Repeat Rows 13 and 14, 4 times.

Rows 23-132: Repeat Rows 3-22, 5 times; then repeat Rows 3-12 once **more**.

Row 133: With **right** side facing, join Lt Green with sc in first sc; (ch 1, sc in next sc) 4 times, ★ ch 1, (sc in next ch-1 sp, ch 1) 4 times, skip next sc, sc in next sc, (ch 1, sc in next sc) 4 times; repeat from ★ across; finish off: 86 sc and 85 ch-1 sps.

TRIM

FIRST SIDE

With **right** side facing, join Lt Green with slip st in first sc on Row 133; slip st in next ch-1 sp, (ch 1, slip st in next ch-1 sp) across to last sc, slip st in last sc; finish off.

SECOND SIDE

With **right** side facing and working in free loops ***(Fig. 2, page 69)*** and in sps across beginning ch, join Lt Green with slip st in first ch; slip st in next sp, (ch 1, slip st in next sp) across to ch at base of last sc, slip st in ch at base of last sc; finish off.

Holding 2 strands of corresponding color yarn together, each 17" (43 cm) long, add additional fringe in each row across short edges of Afghan ***(Figs. 6a & b, page 69)***.

Kid's Play

Finished Size: 44" x 61" (112 cm x 155 cm)

MATERIALS

Worsted Weight Yarn:
- White - 36 ounces, 2,175 yards (1,020 grams, 1,989 meters)
- Red - 4 ounces, 240 yards (110 grams, 219.5 meters)
- Green - 4 ounces, 240 yards (110 grams, 219.5 meters)
- Blue - 4 ounces, 240 yards (110 grams, 219.5 meters)
- Yellow - 4 ounces, 240 yards (110 grams, 219.5 meters)

Crochet hook, size I (5.5 mm) **or** size needed for gauge

Yarn needle

GAUGE SWATCH: $4^1/_4$" (10.75 cm) square
Work same as Square.

STITCH GUIDE

BOBBLE
Ch 3, YO twice, insert hook in third ch from hook, YO and pull up a loop, (YO and draw through 2 loops on hook) twice, YO twice, insert hook in same ch, YO and pull up a loop, (YO and draw through 2 loops on hook) twice, YO and draw through all 5 loops on hook.

CLUSTER
Ch 3, YO, insert hook in third ch from hook, YO and pull up a loop, YO and draw through 2 loops on hook, YO, insert hook in same ch, YO and pull up a loop, YO and draw through 2 loops on hook, YO and draw through all 3 loops on hook.

SQUARE (Make 117)

Referring to the table below, make the number of each Square in the colors indicated.

	Square A	Square B	Square C	Square D
Make	32	31	27	27
Ring & Rnd 1	Red	Green	Blue	Yellow

With color indicated, ch 6; join with slip st to form a ring.

Rnd 1 (Wrong side)**:** Ch 1, (sc in ring, work Bobble) 4 times; join with slip st to first sc, finish off: 4 Bobbles.

Note: Loop a short piece of yarn around **back** of any Bobble on Rnd 1 to mark **right** side.

Rnd 2: With **right** side facing, join White with sc in any sc ***(see Joining With Sc, page 68)***; working **behind** next Bobble ***(Fig. 4, page 69)***, (dc, ch 3, dc) in ring (between sc), ★ sc in next sc, working **behind** next Bobble, (dc, ch 3, dc) in ring; repeat from ★ 2 times **more**; join with slip st to first sc: 12 sts and 4 ch-3 sps.

Rnd 3: Ch 3 **(counts as first dc, now and throughout)**, dc in next dc, (2 dc, ch 3, 2 dc) in next corner ch-3 sp, ★ dc in next 3 sts, (2 dc, ch 3, 2 dc) in next corner ch-3 sp; repeat from ★ 2 times **more**, dc in last dc; join with slip st to first dc: 28 dc and 4 ch-3 sps.

Rnd 4: Ch 3, dc in next 3 dc, (2 dc, ch 3, 2 dc) in next corner ch-3 sp, ★ dc in next 7 dc, (2 dc, ch 3, 2 dc) in next corner ch-3 sp; repeat from ★ 2 times **more**, dc in last 3 dc; join with slip st to first dc, finish off: 44 dc and 4 ch-3 sps.

Continued on page 30.

Ben

ASSEMBLY

With White and using Placement Diagram as a guide, whipstitch Squares together forming 9 vertical strips of 13 Squares each ***(Fig. 5, page 69)***, beginning in second ch of first corner ch-3 and ending in second ch of next corner ch-3; then whipstitch strips together in same manner.

PLACEMENT DIAGRAM

A	B	A	B	A	B	A	B	A
C	D	C	D	C	D	C	D	C
B	A	B	A	B	A	B	A	B
D	C	D	C	D	C	D	C	D
A	B	A	B	A	B	A	B	A
C	D	C	D	C	D	C	D	C
B	A	B	A	B	A	B	A	B
D	C	D	C	D	C	D	C	D
A	B	A	B	A	B	A	B	A
C	D	C	D	C	D	C	D	C
B	A	B	A	B	A	B	A	B
D	C	D	C	D	C	D	C	D
A	B	A	B	A	B	A	B	A

EDGING

Rnd 1: With **wrong** side facing, join Red with sc in any corner ch-3 sp; (work Cluster, ch 1, sc) in same sp, ★ † work Cluster, (skip next 3 dc, sc in next dc, work Cluster) twice, skip next 3 dc, [sc in next sp, work Cluster, skip next joining, sc in next sp, work Cluster, skip next 3 dc, (sc in next dc, work Cluster, skip next 3 dc) twice] across to next corner ch-3 sp †, (sc, work Cluster, ch 1, sc) in corner ch-3 sp; repeat from ★ 2 times **more**, then repeat from † to † once; join with slip st to first sc, finish off: 176 sc and 176 Clusters.

Rnd 2: With **right** side facing and working **behind** any corner Cluster, join White with dc in corner ch-3 sp one rnd **below** (between sc) ***(see Joining With Dc, page 68)***; ★ † sc in next sc on Rnd 1, (ch 1, working **behind** next Cluster, dc in center dc one rnd **below**, ch 1, sc in next sc on Rnd 1) 3 times, [ch 1, working **behind** next Cluster, dc in joining one rnd **below**, ch 1, sc in next sc on Rnd 1, ch 1, working **behind** next Cluster, dc in center dc one rnd **below**, ch 1, sc in next sc on Rnd 1) 3 times] across to next corner Cluster †, working **behind** corner Cluster, (dc, ch 3, dc) in corner ch-3 sp one rnd **below** (between sc); repeat from ★ 2 times **more**, then repeat from † to † once, working **behind** first corner Cluster, dc in same corner ch-3 sp as first dc, ch 3; join with slip st to first dc, finish off: 700 sts and 4 ch-3 sps.

Rnd 3: With **wrong** side facing, join Green with sc in any corner ch-3 sp; (work Cluster, ch 1, sc) in same sp, ★ † work Cluster, skip next 3 sts, (sc in next dc, work Cluster, skip next 3 sts) across to next corner ch-3 sp †, (sc, work Cluster, ch 1, sc) in corner ch-3 sp; repeat from ★ 2 times **more**, then repeat from † to † once; join with slip st to first sc, finish off: 180 sc and 180 Clusters.

Rnd 4: With **right** side facing and working **behind** any corner Cluster, join White with dc in corner ch-3 sp one rnd **below** (between sc); ★ † sc in next sc on previous rnd, (ch 1, working **behind** next Cluster, dc in skipped sc one rnd **below**, ch 1, sc in next sc on previous rnd) across to next corner ch-3 sp †, working **behind** corner Cluster, (dc, ch 3, dc) in corner ch-3 sp one rnd **below** (between sc); repeat from ★ 2 times **more**, then repeat from † to † once, working **behind** first corner Cluster, dc in same corner ch-3 sp as first dc, ch 3; join with slip st to first dc, finish off: 716 sts and 4 ch-3 sps.

Rnd 5: With Yellow, repeat Rnd 3: 184 sc and 184 Clusters.

Rnd 6: Repeat Rnd 4: 732 sts and 4 ch-3 sps.

Rnd 7: With Blue, repeat Rnd 3: 188 sc and 188 Clusters.

Rnd 8: Repeat Rnd 4; do **not** finish off: 380 sts and 372 sps.

Rnd 9: ★ † (Ch 2, slip st in next ch-1 sp) across to within 2 sts of next corner ch-3 sp, ch 2, skip next sc, slip st in next dc, ch 2, slip st in corner ch-3 sp, ch 2 †, slip st in next dc; repeat from ★ 2 times **more**, then repeat from † to † once; join with slip st to same st as joining, finish off.

Lap of Luxury

Finished Size: 50" x 69$^{1}/_{2}$"
(127 cm x 176.5 cm)

MATERIALS

Worsted Weight Yarn:
50 ounces, 2,715 yards
(1,420 grams, 2,482.5 meters)
Crochet hook, size I (5.5 mm) **or** size needed for gauge
Yarn needle

GAUGE: Each Square = 6$^{1}/_{2}$" (16.5 cm)

Gauge Swatch: 4" (10 cm) square
Work same as Square through Rnd 4.

STITCH GUIDE

BEGINNING CLUSTER (uses next 5 dc)
Ch 2, ★ YO, insert hook in **next** dc, YO and pull up a loop, YO and draw through 2 loops on hook; repeat from ★ 4 times **more**, YO and draw through all 6 loops on hook.

CLUSTER (uses next 6 dc)
★ YO, insert hook in **next** dc, YO and pull up a loop, YO and draw through 2 loops on hook; repeat from ★ 5 times **more**, YO and draw through all 7 loops on hook.

SQUARE (Make 70)

Rnd 1 (Wrong side)**:** Ch 2, 8 sc in second ch from hook; join with slip st to Back Loop Only of first sc ***(Fig. 1, page 68)***.

Note: Loop a short piece of yarn around the **back** of any stitch on Rnd 1 to mark **right** side.

Rnd 2: Ch 3 **(counts as first dc, now and throughout)**, 5 dc in same st, ch 3, skip next sc, ★ 6 dc in Back Loop Only of next sc, ch 3, skip next sc; repeat from ★ 2 times **more**; join with slip st to **both** loops of first dc: 24 dc and 4 ch-3 sps.

Rnd 3: Work Beginning Cluster, ch 2, (dc, ch 3, dc) in next corner ch-3 sp, ch 2, ★ work Cluster, ch 2, (dc, ch 3, dc) in next corner ch-3 sp, ch 2; repeat from ★ 2 times **more**; join with slip st to top of Beginning Cluster: 4 Clusters and 12 sps.

Rnd 4: Ch 3, **turn**; 2 dc in next ch-2 sp, dc in next dc, (2 dc, ch 3, 2 dc) in next corner ch-3 sp, dc in next dc, ★ (2 dc in next ch-2 sp, dc in next st) twice, (2 dc, ch 3, 2 dc) in next corner ch-3 sp, dc in next dc; repeat from ★ 2 times **more**, 2 dc in last ch-2 sp; join with slip st to first dc: 44 dc and 4 ch-3 sps.

Rnd 5: Ch 5 **(counts as first dc plus ch 2, now and throughout)**, do **not** turn; skip next 2 dc, dc in next dc, ch 2, skip next 2 dc, (2 dc, ch 3, 2 dc) in next corner ch-3 sp, ch 2, ★ skip next 2 dc, (dc in next dc, ch 2, skip next 2 dc) 3 times, (2 dc, ch 3, 2 dc) in next corner ch-3 sp, ch 2; repeat from ★ 2 times **more**, skip next 2 dc, dc in next dc, ch 2, skip last 2 dc; join with slip st to first dc: 28 dc and 20 sps.

Rnd 6: Ch 5, dc in next dc, ch 2, dc in next 2 dc, (2 dc, ch 3, 2 dc) in next corner ch-3 sp, dc in next 2 dc, ch 2, ★ (dc in next dc, ch 2) 3 times, dc in next 2 dc, (2 dc, ch 3, 2 dc) in next corner ch-3 sp, dc in next 2 dc, ch 2; repeat from ★ 2 times **more**, dc in next dc, ch 2; join with slip st to first dc, finish off: 44 dc and 20 sps.

ASSEMBLY

Whipstitch Squares together forming 7 vertical strips of 10 Squares each ***(Fig. 5, page 69)***, beginning in center ch of first corner ch-3 and ending in center ch of next corner ch-3; then whipstitch strips together in same manner.

EDGING

Rnd 1: With **right** side facing, join yarn with dc in any corner ch-3 sp ***(see Joining With Dc, page 68)***; dc in same sp, ★ † dc in next 4 dc, ch 2, (dc in next dc, ch 2) 3 times, dc in next 4 dc, [ch 2, dc in next joining, ch 2, dc in next 4 dc, ch 2, (dc in next dc, ch 2) 3 times, dc in next 4 dc] across to next corner ch-3 sp †, (2 dc, ch 3, 2 dc) in corner ch-3 sp; repeat from ★ 2 times **more**, then repeat from † to † once, 2 dc in same sp as first dc, ch 1, hdc in first dc to form last corner ch-3 sp: 420 dc and 200 sps.

Rnd 2: Ch 3, dc in last ch-3 sp made, ★ † dc in next 6 dc, ch 2, (dc in next dc, ch 2) 3 times, [dc in next 2 dc, ch 2, skip next 2 dc, 2 dc in next ch-2 sp, dc in next dc, 2 dc in next ch-2 sp, ch 2, skip next 2 dc, dc in next 2 dc, ch 2, (dc in next dc, ch 2) 3 times] across to within 6 dc of next corner ch-3 sp, dc in next 6 dc †, (2 dc, ch 3, 2 dc) in next corner ch-3 sp; repeat from ★ 2 times **more**, then repeat from † to † once, 2 dc in same sp as first dc, ch 1, hdc in first dc to form last corner ch-3 sp: 436 dc and 200 sps.

Rnd 3: Ch 3, dc in last ch-3 sp made, ★ † ch 2, skip next 2 dc, (dc in next dc, ch 2, skip next 2 dc) twice, 2 dc in next ch-2 sp, (dc in next dc, 2 dc in next ch-2 sp) 3 times, [ch 2, skip next 2 dc, 2 dc in next ch-2 sp, dc in next 5 dc, 2 dc in next ch-2 sp, ch 2, skip next 2 dc, 2 dc in next ch-2 sp, (dc in next dc, 2 dc in next ch-2 sp) 3 times] across to within 8 dc of next corner ch-3 sp, ch 2, skip next 2 dc, (dc in next dc, ch 2, skip next 2 dc) twice †, (2 dc, ch 3, 2 dc) in next corner ch-3 sp; repeat from ★ 2 times **more**, then repeat from † to † once, 2 dc in same sp as first dc, ch 1, hdc in first dc to form last corner ch-3 sp: 676 dc and 88 sps.

Rnd 4: Ch 3, dc in last ch-3 sp made and in next dc, ★ † ch 2, (dc in next ch-2 sp, ch 2) 3 times, skip next 2 dc, (dc in next dc, ch 2, skip next 2 dc) 3 times, [dc in next ch-2 sp, ch 2, skip next dc, dc in next dc, ch 2, (skip next 2 dc, dc in next dc, ch 2) twice, skip next dc, dc in next ch-2 sp, ch 2, skip next 2 dc, (dc in next dc, ch 2, skip next 2 dc) 3 times] across to within 3 ch-2 sps of next corner ch-3 sp, (dc in next ch-2 sp, ch 2) 3 times, skip next dc, dc in next dc †, (2 dc, ch 3, 2 dc) in corner ch-3 sp, dc in next dc; repeat from ★ 2 times **more**, then repeat from † to † once, 2 dc in same sp as first dc, dc in first dc to form last corner ch-3 sp: 300 dc and 284 sps.

Rnd 5: (Slip st, ch 1, dc, ch 1, slip st, ch 2, dc) in last ch-3 sp made, ★ † skip next 2 dc, (slip st, ch 2, dc) in next dc and in each dc across to within 2 dc of next corner ch-3 sp, skip next 2 dc †, (slip st, ch 1, dc, ch 1, slip st, ch 2, dc) in corner ch-3 sp; repeat from ★ 2 times **more**, then repeat from † to † once; join with slip st to first slip st, finish off.

Mile-a-Minute Magic

Finished Size: 50" x 70" (127 cm x 178 cm)

MATERIALS

Worsted Weight Yarn:
White - 18 ounces, 950 yards (510 grams, 868.5 meters)
Dk Blue - 14 ounces, 740 yards (400 grams, 676.5 meters)
Blue - 13 ounces, 690 yards (370 grams, 631 meters)
Crochet hook, size I (5.5 mm) **or** size needed for gauge
Yarn needle

GAUGE: In pattern,
4 Cross Sts = 4" (10 cm)
One Strip = 4$^{1}/_{2}$"w x 68"h (11.5 cm x 172.5 cm)

Gauge Swatch: 4$^{1}/_{2}$"w x 10"h (11.5 cm x 25.5 cm)
With White, ch 16.
Work same as Strip.

STITCH GUIDE

TREBLE CROCHET *(abbreviated tr)*
YO twice, insert hook in st or sp indicated, YO and pull up a loop (4 loops on hook), (YO and draw through 2 loops on hook) 3 times.

CROSS ST
Skip next tr, tr in next tr, ch 1, working in **front** of last tr made, tr in skipped tr.

STRIP (Make 11)

With White, ch 220.

Foundation Row (Right side)**:** Sc in fourth ch from hook, ch 1, ★ skip next ch, sc in next ch, ch 1; repeat from ★ across to last 2 chs, skip next ch, (sc, ch 3, slip st) in last ch: 109 sc and 108 ch-1 sps.

Rnd 1: Working in sps across beginning ch, slip st in next sp, ch 5 **(counts as first tr plus ch 1, now and throughout)**, working in **front** of last tr made ***(Fig. 4, page 69)***, tr in last ch made on Foundation Row, ch 1, tr in next sp, ch 1, working in **front** of last tr made, tr in same sp as first tr, ch 1, (skip next sp, tr in next sp, ch 1, working in **front** of last tr made, tr in skipped sp, ch 1) across to ch at base of last sc, skip ch at base of last sc, tr in next ch, ch 1, working in **front** of last tr made, tr in sp before last tr made, ch 1, place marker around ch-1 just made for st placement, (tr in next ch, ch 1, working in **front** of last tr made, tr in ch before last tr made, ch 1) twice; working in ch-1 sps across opposite side of Foundation Row, tr in next ch-1 sp, ch 1, working in **front** of last tr made, tr in ch before last tr made, ch 1, tr in next ch-1 sp, ch 1, working in **front** of last tr made, tr in sp before last tr made, ch 1, (skip next ch-1 sp, tr in next ch-1 sp, ch 1, working in **front** of last tr made, tr in skipped sp, ch 1) across to last sc, skip last sc, tr in next ch, ch 1, working in **front** of last tr made, tr in sp before last tr made, ch 1, place marker around ch-1 just made for st placement, tr in next ch, ch 1, working in **front** of last tr made, tr in ch before last tr made, ch 1, tr in same st as second tr made on beginning of rnd, ch 1, working in **front** of last tr made, tr in ch before last tr made, ch 1; join with slip st to first tr, finish off: 232 tr.

Rnd 2: With **right** side facing, skip first ch-1 sp and join Blue with slip st in next tr; ch 5, working in **front** of last tr made, tr in same st as joining at end of Rnd 1, ch 1, † (work Cross St, ch 1) across to marked ch, skip marked ch, tr in next tr, ch 1, working in **front** of tr just made, tr in tr before last tr made, ch 1, place marker around ch-1 just made for st placement †, (tr in next tr, ch 1, working in **front** of tr just made, tr in tr before last tr made, ch 1) 5 times, repeat from † to † once, (tr in next tr, ch 1, working in **front** of tr just made, tr in tr before last tr, ch 1) 3 times, tr in same st as second tr made at beginning of rnd, ch 1, working in **front** of tr just made, tr in tr before last tr made, ch 1; join with slip st to first tr, finish off: 122 Cross Sts.

Rnd 3: With **right** side facing, skip first ch-1 sp and join Dk Blue with slip st in next tr; ch 5, working in **front** of tr just made, tr in same st as joining at end of Rnd 2, ch 1, ★ (work Cross St, ch 1) across to marked ch, place marker in last tr

made for joining placement, work Cross St, ch 1, (tr in next tr, ch 1, working in **front** of tr just made, tr in tr before last tr, ch 1) 4 times, work Cross St, place marker in first tr of Cross St just made for joining placement, ch 1, working in **front** of tr just made, tr in skipped tr, ch 1; repeat from ★ once **more**; join with slip st to first tr, finish off: 126 Cross Sts.

ASSEMBLY

Remove markers as Strips are joined, leaving markers on outer Strips for Edging placement.

Holding two Strips together and using Dk Blue, whipstitch Strips together ***(Fig. 5, page 69)***, beginning in first marked tr and ending in next marked tr.

EDGING

With **right** side facing, join Dk Blue with slip st in first ch-1 sp after marked tr in top corner; † ★ (ch 1, slip st in next ch-1 sp) across to next joining, skip joining, slip st in next ch-1 sp; repeat from ★ 9 times **more** †; repeat from † to † once, ch 1, (slip st in next ch-1 sp, ch 1) across; join with slip st to first slip st, finish off.

No-nonsense Accents

Finished Size: 48" x $68^{1}/_{2}$" (122 cm x 174 cm)

MATERIALS

Worsted Weight Yarn:
- Black - 40 ounces, 2,260 yards (1,140 grams, 2,066.5 meters)
- Yellow - $8^{1}/_{4}$ ounces, 465 yards (235 grams, 425 meters)
- Rose - 8 ounces, 450 yards (230 grams, 411.5 meters)
- Blue - 8 ounces, 450 yards (230 grams, 411.5 meters)
- Teal - 8 ounces, 450 yards (230 grams, 411.5 meters)

Crochet hook, size I (5.5 mm) **or** size needed for gauge

GAUGE: In pattern,
13 sts and 14 rows = 4" (10 cm)

Gauge Swatch: 7"w x 4"h (17.75 cm x 10 cm)
With Black, ch 24.
Work same as Afghan Body for 14 rows.

Each row is worked across length of Afghan. When joining yarn and finishing off, leave a 9" (23 cm) end to be worked into fringe.

AFGHAN BODY

With Black, ch 224.

Row 1 (Right side): Sc in second ch from hook and in each ch across; finish off: 223 sc.

Note: Loop a short piece of yarn around any stitch to mark Row 1 as **right** side.

Row 2: With **wrong** side facing, join Yellow with sc in first sc ***(see Joining With Sc, page 68)***; sc in next sc, ch 3, ★ skip next 3 sc, sc in next 5 sts, ch 3; repeat from ★ across to last 5 sc, skip next 3 sc, sc in last 2 sc; finish off: 139 sc and 28 ch-3 sps.

Row 3: With **right** side facing, join Black with sc in first sc; ch 1, skip next sc, working in **front** of next ch-3 ***(Fig. 4, page 69)***, dc in next 3 skipped sc one row **below**, ch 1, ★ skip next sc on Row 2, sc in next 3 sc, ch 1, skip next sc, working in **front** of next ch-3, dc in next 3 skipped sc one row **below**, ch 1; repeat from ★ across to last 2 sc on Row 2, skip next sc, sc in last sc; finish off: 167 sts and 56 ch-1 sps.

Row 4: With **wrong** side facing, join Yellow with sc in first sc; working **behind** next ch-1, dc in skipped sc one row **below**, sc in next 3 dc on Row 3, working **behind** next ch-1, dc in skipped sc one row **below**, ★ ch 3, skip next 3 sc on Row 3, working **behind** next ch-1, dc in skipped sc one row **below**, sc in next 3 dc on Row 3, working **behind** next ch-1, dc in skipped sc one row **below**; repeat from ★ across to last sc, sc in last sc; finish off: 142 sts and 27 ch-3 sps.

Row 5: With **right** side facing, join Black with sc in first sc; ★ sc in next 5 sts on Row 4, working in **front** of next ch-3, dc in next 3 skipped sc one row **below**; repeat from ★ across to last 6 sts, sc in last 6 sts; finish off: 223 sts.

Rows 6-165: Repeat Rows 2-5 for pattern, working in the following color sequence: ★ 1 row **each** of (Rose, Black) twice, (Blue, Black) twice, (Teal, Black) twice, (Yellow, Black) twice; repeat from ★ 9 times **more**.

TRIM

FIRST SIDE

Row 1: With **wrong** side facing, join Black with sc in first sc on Row 165; sc in next sc, ch 1, ★ skip next st, sc in next st, ch 1; repeat from ★ across to last 3 sc, skip next sc, sc in last 2 sc.

Row 2: Ch 1, turn; slip st in first sc, ch 2, (slip st in next ch-1 sp, ch 2) across, skip next sc, slip st in last sc; finish off.

SECOND SIDE

Row 1: With **wrong** side facing and working in free loops of beginning ch ***(Fig. 2, page 69)***, join Black with sc in ch at base of first sc; sc in next ch, ch 1, ★ skip next ch, sc in next ch, ch 1; repeat from ★ across to last 3 chs, skip next ch, sc in last 2 chs.

Row 2: Ch 1, turn; slip st in first sc, ch 2, (slip st in next ch-1 sp, ch 2) across, skip next sc, slip st in last sc; finish off.

Holding 2 strands of corresponding color yarn together, each 19" (48.5 cm) long, add additional fringe in each row across short edges of Afghan ***(Figs. 6a & b, page 69)***.

One-of-a-kind

Finished Size: 56" x 74" (142 cm x 188 cm)

MATERIALS

Bulky Weight Yarn:
  Ecru - 77 ounces, 2,180 yards (2,190 grams, 1,993.5 meters)
  Blue - 28 ounces, 795 yards (800 grams, 727 meters)
Crochet hook, size J (6 mm) **or** size needed for gauge
Safety pin
Yarn needle

GAUGE: Each Square = 6" (15.25 cm)

Gauge Swatch: 3" (7.5 cm) square
Work same as Square through Rnd 2.

STITCH GUIDE

TREBLE CROCHET *(abbreviated tr)*
YO twice, insert hook in st or sp indicated, YO and pull up a loop (4 loops on hook), (YO and draw through 2 loops on hook) 3 times.

SQUARE (Make 88)

With Ecru, ch 5; join with slip st to form a ring.

Rnd 1 (Right side)**:** Ch 3 **(counts as first dc, now and throughout)**, 2 dc in ring, (ch 3, 3 dc in ring) 3 times, ch 1, hdc in first dc to form last ch-3 sp: 12 dc.

Note: Loop a short piece of yarn around any stitch to mark Rnd 1 as **right** side.

Rnd 2: Ch 5 **(counts as first tr plus ch 1, now and throughout)**, 2 dc in last ch-3 sp made, dc in next 3 dc, ★ (2 dc, ch 1, tr, ch 1, 2 dc) in next ch-3 sp, dc in next 3 dc; repeat from ★ around, 2 dc in same sp as first tr, ch 1; join with slip st to first tr; place loop from hook onto safety pin to keep piece from unraveling as you work the next rnd: 28 dc and 4 tr.

Rnd 3: With **wrong** side facing and keeping safety pin and working yarn on **wrong** side of work, join Blue with sc in ch before any corner tr ***(see Joining With Sc, page 68)***; ch 3, skip corner tr, sc in next ch, ch 1, skip next dc, (sc in next dc, ch 1, skip next dc) 3 times, ★ sc in next ch, ch 3, skip next corner tr, sc in next ch, ch 1, skip next dc, (sc in next dc, ch 1, skip next dc) 3 times; repeat from ★ 2 times **more**; join with slip st to first sc, finish off: 20 sc and 20 sps.

Rnd 4: With **right** side facing and working **behind** corner ch-3, remove safety pin and place Ecru loop onto hook; ch 5, dc in same st as joining on Rnd 2 ***(Fig. 4, page 69)***, ch 1, skip next sc on Rnd 3, ★ † working in **front** of next ch-1, dc in skipped dc one rnd **below**, (sc in next sc on Rnd 3, working in **front** of next ch-1, dc in skipped dc one rnd **below**) 3 times, ch 1, skip next sc on Rnd 3 †, working **behind** next corner ch-3, (dc, ch 1, tr, ch 1, dc) in corner tr one rnd **below**, ch 1, skip next sc on Rnd 3; repeat from ★ 2 times **more**, then repeat from † to † once, working **behind** corner ch-3, dc in same corner tr as first tr, ch 1; join with slip st to first tr, place loop from hook onto safety pin: 40 sts and 16 ch-1 sps.

Rnd 5: With **wrong** side facing and keeping safety pin and working yarn on **right** side of work, join Blue with sc in ch before any corner tr; ★ † ch 3, skip corner tr, sc in next ch, ch 1, skip next dc, working **behind** next ch-1, dc in skipped sc one rnd **below**, ch 1, skip next dc on Rnd 4, (sc in next sc, ch 1, skip next dc) 3 times, working **behind** next ch-1, dc in skipped sc one rnd **below**, ch 1, skip next dc on Rnd 4 †, sc in next ch; repeat from ★ 2 times **more**, then repeat from † to † once; join with slip st to first sc, finish off: 28 sts and 28 sps.

Continued on page 40.

Rnd 6: With **right** side facing and working in **front** of corner ch-3, remove safety pin and place Ecru loop onto hook; ch 3, ★ † sc in next sc on Rnd 5, working in **front** of next ch-1, dc in skipped dc one rnd **below**, sc in next dc on Rnd 5, (working **behind** next ch-1, dc in skipped dc one rnd **below**, sc in next st on Rnd 5) 4 times, working in **front** of next ch-1, dc in skipped dc one rnd **below**, sc in next sc on Rnd 5 †, working in **front** of next corner ch-3, (dc, ch 3, dc) in corner tr one rnd **below**; repeat from ★ 2 times **more**, then repeat from † to † once, working in **front** of corner ch-3, dc in same st as first dc, ch 3; join with slip st to first dc, finish off: 60 sts and 4 ch-3 sps.

ASSEMBLY

With Ecru, whipstitch Squares together forming 8 vertical strips of 11 Squares each *(Fig. 5, page 69)*, beginning in center ch of first corner ch-3 and ending in center ch of next corner ch-3; then whipstitch strips together in same manner.

EDGING

When working into chains, work into top 2 loops of **each** chain *(Fig. 3, page 69)*.

Rnd 1: With **right** side facing, join Ecru with dc in any corner ch-3 sp *(see Joining With Dc, page 68)*; (dc, ch 1, tr, ch 1, 2 dc) in same sp, ★ † dc in next 15 sts, (dc in next ch, dc in joining and in next ch, dc in next 15 sts) across to next corner ch-3 sp †, (2 dc, ch 1, tr, ch 1, 2 dc) in corner ch-3 sp; repeat from ★ 2 times **more**, then repeat from † to † once; join with slip st to first dc, finish off: 692 sts and 8 ch-1 sps.

Rnd 2: With **wrong** side facing, join Blue with sc in ch before any corner tr; ★ † ch 3, skip corner tr, sc in next ch, ch 1, skip next dc, (sc in next dc, ch 1, skip next dc) across to next corner †, sc in next ch; repeat from ★ 2 times **more**, then repeat from † to † once; join with slip st to first sc, finish off: 350 sc and 350 sps.

Rnd 3: With **right** side facing, join Ecru with sc in same sc as joining slip st; ★ † (working **behind** next ch-1, dc in skipped dc one rnd **below**, sc in next sc on Rnd 2) across to next corner ch-3, working **behind** corner ch-3, (dc, ch 1, tr, ch 1, dc) in corner tr one rnd **below** †, sc in next sc on Rnd 2; repeat from ★ 2 times **more**, then repeat from † to † once; join with slip st to first sc, finish off: 708 sts and 8 sps.

Rnd 4: With **wrong** side facing, join Blue with sc in ch before any corner tr; ★ † ch 3, skip corner tr, sc in next ch, ch 1, skip next dc, (sc in next sc, ch 1, skip next dc) across to next corner †, sc in next ch; repeat from ★ 2 times **more**, then repeat from † to † once; join with slip st to first sc, finish off: 358 sc and 358 sps.

Rnd 5: With **right** side facing, join Ecru with sc in sc before any corner ch-3; ★ † working in **front** of corner ch-3, (dc, ch 1, tr, ch 1, dc) in corner tr one rnd **below**, [(sc in next sc on Rnd 4, working in **front** of next ch-1, dc in skipped dc one rnd **below**) 4 times, ch 1, skip next sc on Rnd 4, working **behind** next ch-1, dc in skipped dc one rnd **below**, (sc in next sc on Rnd 4, working **behind** next ch-1, dc in skipped dc one rnd **below**) 3 times, ch 1, skip next sc on Rnd 4, working in **front** of next ch-1, dc in skipped dc one rnd **below**] across to within 3 ch-1 sps of next corner ch-3, (sc in next sc on Rnd 4, working in **front** of next ch-1, dc in skipped dc one rnd **below**) 3 times †, sc in next sc on Rnd 4; repeat from ★ 2 times **more**, then repeat from † to † once; join with slip st to first sc, finish off: 724 sts and 8 sps.

Rnd 6: With **wrong** side facing, join Blue with sc in ch after any corner tr; ★ † ch 1, skip next dc, (sc in next sc, ch 1, skip next dc) 4 times, [working **behind** next ch-1, dc in skipped sc one rnd **below**, ch 1, skip next dc on Rnd 5, (sc in next sc, ch 1, skip next dc) 3 times, working **behind** next ch-1, dc in skipped sc one rnd **below**, ch 1, skip next dc on Rnd 5, (sc in next sc, ch 1, skip next dc) 4 times] across to next corner, sc in next ch, ch 3, skip corner tr †, sc in next ch; repeat from ★ 2 times **more**, then repeat from † to † once; join with slip st to first sc, finish off: 366 sts and 366 sps.

Rnd 7: With **right** side facing, join Ecru with sc in sc before any corner ch-3; ★ † working **behind** corner ch-3, (dc, ch 1, tr, ch 1, dc) in corner tr one rnd **below**, (sc in next sc on Rnd 6, working **behind** next ch-1, dc in skipped dc one rnd **below**) 5 times, [ch 1, skip next dc on Rnd 6, working in **front** of next ch-1, dc in skipped dc one rnd **below**, (sc in next sc on Rnd 6, working in **front** of next ch-1, dc in skipped dc one rnd **below**) 3 times, ch 1, skip next dc on Rnd 6, working **behind** next ch-1, dc in skipped dc one rnd **below**, (sc in next sc on Rnd 6, working **behind** next ch-1, dc in skipped dc one rnd **below**) 4 times] across to within one sc of next corner ch-3 †, sc in next sc; repeat from ★ 2 times **more**, then repeat from † to † once; join with slip st to first sc, finish off: 740 sts and 8 sps.

Rnd 8: With **wrong** side facing, join Blue with sc in ch before any corner tr; ★ † ch 3, skip corner tr, sc in next ch, ch 1, skip next dc, (sc in next sc, ch 1, skip next dc) 5 times, working **behind** next ch-1, dc in skipped dc one rnd **below**, ch 1, skip next dc on Rnd 7, (sc in next sc, ch 1, skip next dc) 3 times, working **behind** next ch-1, dc in skipped dc one rnd **below**, ch 1, [skip next dc on Rnd 7, (sc in next sc, ch 1, skip next dc) 4 times, working **behind** next ch-1, dc in skipped dc one rnd **below**, ch 1, skip next dc on Rnd 7, (sc in next sc, ch 1, skip next dc) 3 times, working **behind** next ch-1, dc in skipped dc one rnd **below**, ch 1] across to within 11 sts of first ch-1 of next corner, skip next dc, (sc in next sc, ch 1, skip next dc) 5 times †, sc in next ch; repeat from ★ 2 times **more**, then repeat from † to † once; join with slip st to first sc, finish off: 374 sts and 374 sps.

Rnd 9: With **right** side facing, join Ecru with sc in sc before any corner ch-3 sp; ★ † working in **front** of corner ch-3, (dc, ch 1, tr, ch 1, dc) in corner tr one rnd **below**, (sc in next sc on Rnd 8, working in **front** of next ch-1, dc in skipped dc one rnd **below**) 6 times, (sc in next st on Rnd 8, working **behind** next ch-1, dc in skipped dc one rnd **below**) 4 times, [(sc in next st on Rnd 8, working in **front** of next ch-1, dc in skipped dc one rnd **below**) 5 times, (sc in next st on Rnd 8, working **behind** next ch-1, dc in skipped dc one rnd **below**) 4 times] across to within 6 ch-1 sps of next corner ch-3, (sc in next st on Rnd 8, working in **front** of next ch-1, dc in skipped dc one rnd **below**) 6 times †, sc in next sc on Rnd 8; repeat from ★ 2 times **more**, then repeat from † to † once; join with slip st to first sc, finish off: 756 sts and 8 sps.

Rnd 10: With **wrong** side facing, join Blue with sc in ch before any corner tr; ★ † ch 3, skip corner tr, sc in next ch, ch 1, skip next dc, (sc in next sc, ch 1, skip next dc) across to next corner †, sc in next ch; repeat from ★ 2 times **more**, then repeat from † to † once; join with slip st to first sc, finish off: 382 sc and 382 sps.

Rnd 11: With **right** side facing, join Ecru with sc in same sc as joining slip st; ★ † (working **behind** next ch-1, dc in skipped dc one rnd **below**, sc in next sc on Rnd 10) across to next corner ch-3, working **behind** corner ch-3, (dc, ch 1, tr, ch 1, dc) in corner tr one rnd **below** †, sc in next sc on Rnd 10; repeat from ★ 2 times **more**, then repeat from † to † once; join with slip st to first sc, finish off: 772 sts and 8 sps.

Rnd 12: Ch 1, turn; sc in same st as joining, ch 1, skip next dc, sc in next ch, ch 1, sc in next tr, ch 1, sc in next ch, ch 1, ★ skip next dc, (sc in next sc, ch 1, skip next dc) across to next corner ch-1, sc in next ch, ch 1, sc in next tr, ch 1, sc in next ch, ch 1; repeat from ★ 2 times **more**, skip next dc, (sc in next sc, ch 1, skip next dc) across; join with slip st to first sc.

Rnd 13: Ch 1, turn; (slip st in next ch-1 sp, ch 2) around; join with slip st to first slip st, finish off.

Perfectly Pieced

Finished Size: 50" x 65" (127 cm x 165 cm)

MATERIALS

Worsted Weight Yarn:
- Tan - $17^1/_2$ ounces, 1,150 yards (500 grams, 1,051.5 meters)
- Ecru - 17 ounces, 1,120 yards (480 grams, 1,024 meters)
- Black - $16^1/_2$ ounces, 1,080 yards (470 grams, 987.5 meters)

Crochet hook, size I (5.5 mm) **or** size needed for gauge

Yarn needle

GAUGE: Each Square = 5" (12.75 cm)

Gauge Swatch: $2^1/_4$" (5.75 cm) square
Work same as Square through Rnd 3.

STITCH GUIDE

TREBLE CROCHET *(abbreviated tr)*
YO twice, insert hook in sc indicated, YO and pull up a loop (4 loops on hook), (YO and draw through 2 loops on hook) 3 times.

SQUARE

Referring to the table below, make 54 of each Square in the colors indicated.

	Square A	**Square B**
Rnds 1-3	Tan	Ecru
Rnds 4 & 5	Ecru	Tan
Rnds 6 & 7	Tan	Ecru
Rnd 8	Black	Black

Rnd 1: With color indicated, ch 2, (sc, ch 2) 4 times in second ch from hook; join with slip st to first sc: 4 sc and 4 ch-2 sps.

Rnd 2 (Right side)**:** Ch 1, turn; ★ (sc, ch 2, sc) in next ch-2 sp, ch 1; repeat from ★ around; join with slip st to first sc: 8 sc and 8 sps.

Note: Loop a short piece of yarn around any stitch to mark Rnd 2 as **right** side.

Rnd 3: Ch 1, turn; ★ sc in next ch-1 sp, ch 1, (sc, ch 2, sc) in next corner ch-2 sp, ch 1; repeat from ★ around; join with slip st to first sc, finish off: 12 sc and 12 sps.

Rnd 4: With **right** side facing, join color indicated with sc in any corner ch-2 sp ***(see Joining With Sc, page 68)***; ch 2, sc in same sp, ★ † sc in next sc, working in **front** of next ch-1 ***(Fig. 4, page 69)***, dc in skipped sc one rnd **below**, working in **front** of next sc, tr in skipped sc two Lrnds **below**, working in **front** of next ch-1, dc in skipped sc one rnd **below**, sc in next sc on Rnd 3 †, (sc, ch 2, sc) in corner ch-2 sp; repeat from ★ 2 times **more**, then repeat from † to † once; join with slip st to first sc: 28 sts and 4 ch-2 sps.

Continued on page 44.

Rnd 5: Ch 1, turn; ★ (sc in next st, ch 1, skip next st) 3 times, (sc, ch 2, sc) in next corner ch-2 sp, ch 1, skip next sc; repeat from ★ around; join with slip st to first sc, finish off: 20 sc and 20 sps.

Rnd 6: With **right** side facing, join color indicated with sc in first sc after any corner ch-2 sp; ★ † (working **behind** next ch-1, dc in skipped st one rnd **below**, sc in next sc on Rnd 5) 4 times, ch 3, skip corner ch-2 sp †, sc in next sc; repeat from ★ 2 times **more**, then repeat from † to † once; join with slip st to first sc: 36 sts and 4 ch-3 sps.

Rnd 7: Ch 1, turn; ★ (sc, ch 3, sc) in next corner ch-3 sp, ch 1, skip next sc, (sc in next dc, ch 1, skip next sc) 4 times; repeat from ★ around; join with slip st to first sc, finish off: 24 sc and 24 sps.

Rnd 8: With **right** side facing, join color indicated with sc in sc after any corner ch-3 sp; ★ † (working **behind** next ch-1, dc in skipped sc one rnd **below**, sc in next sc on Rnd 7) 5 times, working **behind** next corner ch-3, (dc, ch 3, dc) **between** sc in corner ch-3 sp one rnd **below** †, sc in next sc on Rnd 7; repeat from ★ 2 times **more**, then repeat from † to † once; join with slip st to first sc, finish off: 52 sts and 3 ch-3 sps.

ASSEMBLY

With Black and using Placement Diagram as a guide, whipstitch Squares together forming 9 vertical strips of 12 Squares each ***(Fig. 5, page 69)***, beginning in center ch of first corner ch-3 and ending in center ch of next corner ch-3; then whipstitch strips together in same manner.

PLACEMENT DIAGRAM

A	B	A	B	A	B	A	B	A
B	A	B	A	B	A	B	A	B
A	B	A	B	A	B	A	B	A
B	A	B	A	B	A	B	A	B
A	B	A	B	A	B	A	B	A
B	A	B	A	B	A	B	A	B
A	B	A	B	A	B	A	B	A
B	A	B	A	B	A	B	A	B
A	B	A	B	A	B	A	B	A
B	A	B	A	B	A	B	A	B
A	B	A	B	A	B	A	B	A
B	A	B	A	B	A	B	A	B

EDGING

Rnd 1: With **wrong** side facing, join Black with sc in any corner ch-3 sp; ch 3, sc in same sp,★ † ch 1, skip next dc, (sc in next sc, ch 1, skip next dc) 6 times, [sc in next sp, ch 1, skip joining, sc in next sp, ch 1, skip next dc, (sc in next sc, ch 1, skip next dc) 6 times] across to next corner ch-3 sp †, (sc, ch 3, sc) in corner ch-3 sp; repeat from ★ 2 times **more**, then repeat from † to † once; join with slip st to first sc, finish off: 336 sc and 336 sps.

Rnd 2: With **right** side facing, join Tan with sc in sc after any corner ch-3; ★ † (working **behind** next ch-1, dc in skipped dc one rnd **below**, sc in next sc on Rnd 1) 7 times, [working **behind** next ch-1, dc in joining, sc in next sc on Rnd 1, (working **behind** next ch-1, dc in skipped dc one rnd **below**, sc in next sc on Rnd 1) 7 times] across to next corner ch-3, working **behind** corner ch-3, (dc, ch 3, dc) **between** sc in corner ch-3 sp one rnd **below** †, sc in next sc on Rnd 1; repeat from ★ 2 times **more**, then repeat from † to † once; join with slip st to first sc: 676 sts and 4 ch-3 sps.

Rnd 3: Ch 1, turn; sc in same st as joining, ch 1, skip next dc, (sc, ch 3, sc) in next corner ch-3 sp, ch 1, skip next dc, ★ (sc in next sc, ch 1, skip next dc) across to next corner ch-3 sp, (sc, ch 3, sc) in corner ch-3 sp, ch 1, skip next dc; repeat from ★ 2 times **more**, (sc in next sc, ch 1, skip next dc) across; join with slip st to first sc, finish off: 344 sc and 344 sps.

Rnd 4: With **right** side facing, join Ecru with sc in sc after any corner ch-3; ★ † (working **behind** next ch-1, dc in skipped dc one rnd **below**, sc in next sc) across to next corner ch-3, working **behind** corner ch-3, (dc, ch 3, dc) **between** sc in corner ch-3 sp one rnd **below** †, sc in next sc; repeat from ★ 2 times **more**, then repeat from † to † once; join with slip st to first sc: 692 sts and 4 ch-3 sps.

Rnd 5: Repeat Rnd 3: 352 sc and 352 sps.

Rnd 6: With Tan, repeat Rnd 4: 708 sts and 4 ch-3 sps.

Rnd 7: Repeat Rnd 3: 360 sc and 360 sps.

Rnd 8: With Black, repeat Rnd 4: 724 sts and 4 ch-3 sps.

Rnd 9: Repeat Rnd 3; do **not** finish off: 368 sc and 368 sps.

Rnd 10: Ch 1, turn; ★ † (slip st in next ch-1 sp, ch 1) across to next corner ch-3 sp, (slip st, ch 2, slip st) in corner ch-3 sp, ch 1; repeat from ★ 3 times **more**, slip st in last ch-1 sp, ch 1; join with slip st to first slip st, finish off.

Quiet Quest

Finished Size: 50" x 66½" (127 cm x 169 cm)

MATERIALS

Worsted Weight Yarn:
- Ecru - 47 ounces, 2,380 yards (1,330 grams, 2,176.5 meters)
- Black - 21 ounces, 1,065 yards (600 grams, 974 meters)
- Brown - 19 ounces, 960 yards (540 grams, 878 meters)
- Orange - 16 ounces, 810 yards (450 grams, 740.5 meters)

Crochet hook, size K (6.5 mm) **or** size needed for gauge

Yarn needle

Each row is worked across length of Strip holding two strands of yarn together. When joining yarn and finishing off, leave a 9" (23 cm) end to be worked into fringe.

GAUGE: In pattern, 8 sts = 3" (7.5 cm)
One Strip = 3¾" wide x 67" long (9.5 cm x 170 cm)

Gauge Swatch: 3¾"w x 5"h (9.5 cm x 12.75 cm)
Holding two strands of Ecru together, ch 14.
Work same as Strip.

STITCH GUIDE

TREBLE CROCHET *(abbreviated tr)*
YO twice, insert hook in ch indicated, YO and pull up a loop (4 loops on hook), (YO and draw through 2 loops on hook) 3 times.

STRIP A (Make 7)

Holding two strands of Ecru together, ch 178.

Foundation Row (Wrong side)**:** Sc in second ch from hook and in next ch, ch 1, ★ skip next ch, sc in next ch, ch 1; repeat from ★ across to last 3 chs, skip next ch, sc in last 2 chs; finish off: 90 sc and 87 ch-1 sps.

Note: Loop a short piece of yarn around **back** of last sc made on Foundation Row to mark **right** side and **bottom** edge.

FIRST HALF

Row 1: With **right** side facing and holding two strands of Brown together, join yarn with dc in first sc ***(see Joining With Dc, page 68)***; ★ (dc, ch 1) twice in next ch-1 sp, skip next ch-1 sp; repeat from ★ across to last ch-1 sp, (dc, ch 1, dc) in last ch-1 sp, skip next sc, dc in last sc; finish off: 176 dc and 87 ch-1 sps.

Row 2: With **wrong** side facing and holding two strands of Ecru together, join yarn with sc in first dc ***(see Joining With Sc, page 68)***; ch 1, sc in next ch-1 sp, ch 1, ★ working in **front** of next ch-1 ***(Fig. 4, page 69)***, tr in skipped ch-1 one row **below**, ch 1, sc in next ch-1 sp on Row 1, ch 1; repeat from ★ across to last 2 dc on Row 1, skip next dc, sc in last dc; finish off: 89 sts and 88 ch-1 sps.

Row 3: With **right** side facing and holding two strands of Black together, join yarn with sc in first sc; ★ ch 1, skip next ch, sc in next st; repeat from ★ across; finish off.

SECOND HALF

Row 1: With **right** side facing, holding two strands of Brown together, and working in free loops ***(Fig. 2, page 69)*** and in sps across beginning ch, join yarn with dc in ch at base of first sc; ★ (dc, ch 1) twice in next sp, skip next sp; repeat from ★ across to last sp, (dc, ch 1, dc) in last sp, skip next ch, dc in last ch; finish off: 176 dc and 87 ch-1 sps.

Rows 2 and 3: Work same as First Half: 89 sts and 88 ch-1 sps.

STRIP B (Make 6)

Holding two strands of Ecru together, ch 178.

Foundation Row (Wrong side)**:** Sc in second ch from hook and in next ch, ch 1, ★ skip next ch, sc in next ch, ch 1; repeat from ★ across to last 3 chs, skip next ch, sc in last 2 chs; finish off: 90 sc and 87 ch-1 sps.

Note: Loop a short piece of yarn around **back** of last sc made on Foundation Row to mark **right** side and **bottom** edge.

FIRST HALF

Row 1: With **right** side facing and holding two strands of Orange together, join yarn with dc in first sc; ★ (dc, ch 1) twice in next ch-1 sp, skip next ch-1 sp; repeat from ★ across to last ch-1 sp, (dc, ch 1, dc) in last ch-1 sp, skip next sc, dc in last sc; finish off: 176 sc and 87 ch-1 sps.

Row 2: With **wrong** side facing and holding two strands of Ecru together, join yarn with sc in first dc; ch 1, sc in next ch-1 sp, ch 1, ★ working in **front** of next ch-1, tr in skipped ch-1 one row **below**, ch 1, sc in next ch-1 sp on Row 1, ch 1; repeat from ★ across to last 2 dc on Row 1, skip next dc, sc in last dc; finish off: 89 sts and 88 ch-1 sps.

Row 3: With **right** side facing and holding two strands of Black together, join yarn with sc in first sc; ★ ch 1, skip next ch, sc in next st; repeat from ★ across; finish off.

SECOND HALF

Row 1: With **right** side facing, holding two strands of Orange together, and working in free loops and in sps across beginning ch, join yarn with dc in ch at base of first sc; ★ (dc, ch 1) twice in next sp, skip next sp; repeat from ★ across to last sp, (dc, ch 1, dc) in last sp, skip next ch, dc in last ch; finish off: 176 dc and 87 ch-1 sps.

Rows 2 and 3: Work same as First Half: 89 sts and 88 ch-1 sps.

ASSEMBLY

Holding Strips A and B together with bottom edges at the same end and using one strand of Black, whipstitch Strips together ***(Fig. 5, page 69)***, beginning in first sc and ending in last sc. Join remaining Strips in same manner, alternating Strips A and B.

TRIM

FIRST SIDE

Row 1: With **wrong** side of long edge facing and holding two strands of Black together, join yarn with sc in first sc; sc in next ch-1 sp, (ch 1, sc in next ch-1 sp) across, sc in last sc.

Row 2: Ch 1, turn; slip st in first sc, ch 1, ★ slip st in next ch-1 sp, ch 1, skip next sc; repeat from ★ across to last sc, slip st in last sc; finish off.

SECOND SIDE

Work same as First Side across second long edge.

Holding 4 strands of corresponding color yarn together, each 19" (48.5 cm) long, add additional fringe in each stripe across short edges of Afghan ***(Figs. 6a & b, page 69)***.

Rainbow for Baby

Finished Size: 36" x 48" (91.5 cm x 122 cm)

MATERIALS

Worsted Weight Yarn:
- White - 5½ ounces, 310 yards (160 grams, 283.5 meters)
- Pink - 5 ounces, 285 yards (140 grams, 260.5 meters)
- Peach - 5 ounces, 285 yards (140 grams, 260.5 meters)
- Yellow - 5 ounces, 285 yards (140 grams, 260.5 meters)
- Green - 5 ounces, 285 yards (140 grams, 260.5 meters)
- Blue - 5 ounces, 285 yards (140 grams, 260.5 meters)

Crochet hook, size I (5.5 mm) **or** size needed for gauge

GAUGE: In pattern,
(dc, ch 1, dc) 4 times = 3¼" (8.25 cm);
6 rows = 3½" (9 cm)

Gauge Swatch: 3½" (9 cm) square
With White, ch 16.
Work same as Afghan Body for 6 rows.

Each row is worked across length of Afghan. When joining yarn and finishing off, leave a 7" (18 cm) end to be worked into fringe.

AFGHAN BODY

With White, ch 178, place marker in third ch from hook for st placement.

Row 1 (Right side)**:** (Dc, ch 1, dc) in fifth ch from hook, ★ skip next 2 chs, (dc, ch 1, dc) in next ch; repeat from ★ across to last 2 chs, skip next ch, dc in last ch; finish off: 58 ch-1 sps.

Note: Loop a short piece of yarn around any stitch to mark Row 1 as **right** side.

Row 2: With **wrong** side facing, join Pink with dc in first dc ***(see Joining With Dc, page 68)***; (dc, ch 1, dc) in each ch-1 sp across, skip next dc, dc in next ch; finish off.

Row 3: With **right** side facing, join Peach with dc in first dc; (dc, ch 1, dc) in each ch-1 sp across, skip next dc, dc in last dc; finish off.

Row 4: With **wrong** side facing, join Yellow with dc in first dc; (dc, ch 1, dc) in each ch-1 sp across, skip next dc, dc in last dc; finish off.

Row 5: With **right** side facing, join Green with dc in first dc; (dc, ch 1, dc) in each ch-1 sp across, skip next dc, dc in last dc; finish off.

Row 6: With **wrong** side facing, join Blue with dc in first dc; (dc, ch 1, dc) in each ch-1 sp across, skip next dc, dc in last dc; finish off.

Row 7: With **right** side facing, join White with dc in first dc; (dc, ch 1, dc) in each ch-1 sp across, skip next dc, dc in last dc; finish off.

Row 8: With **wrong** side facing, join Pink with dc in first dc; (dc, ch 1, dc) in each ch-1 sp across, skip next dc, dc in last dc; finish off.

Rows 9-61: Repeat Rows 3-8, 8 times; then repeat Rows 3-7 once **more**.

TRIM

FIRST SIDE

With **right** side facing, join White with slip st in first dc on Row 61; ch 2, slip st in next ch-1 sp, (ch 3, slip st in next ch-1 sp) across, ch 2, skip next dc, slip st in last dc; finish off.

SECOND SIDE

With **right** side facing and working in free loops of beginning ch ***(Fig. 2, page 69)***, join White with slip st in first ch; ch 3, (slip st in next sp, ch 3) across to marked ch, slip st in marked ch; finish off.

Holding 4 strands of corresponding color together, each 15" (38 cm) long, add additional fringe in each row across short edges of Afghan ***(Figs. 6a & b, page 69)***.

Random House

Spring Serenade

Finished Size: 50" x 68" (127 cm x 172.5 cm)

MATERIALS

Worsted Weight Yarn:
- White - 28 ounces, 1,835 yards (800 grams, 1,678 meters)
- Teal - 11 ounces, 720 yards (310 grams, 658.5 meters)

Crochet hook, size I (5.5 mm) **or** size needed for gauge
Yarn needle

GAUGE: In pattern,
(Cluster, ring) 3 times = $4^1/_2$" (11.5 cm);
Each Strip = $4^1/_2$" (11.5 cm) wide

Gauge Swatch: $4^1/_2$"w x $9^1/_2$"h (11.5 cm x 24.25 cm)

Foundation Row (Right side)**:** With White, ch 3, dc in third ch from hook (ring made), ★ work Cluster, ch 3, dc in third ch from hook; repeat from ★ 2 times **more**, ch 1; finish off: 3 Clusters and 4 rings.
Rnds 1-3: Work same as Strip.

STITCH GUIDE

TREBLE CROCHET *(abbreviated tr)*
YO twice, insert hook in sp indicated, YO and pull up a loop (4 loops on hook), (YO and draw through 2 loops on hook) 3 times.

CLUSTER
Ch 3, YO, insert hook in third ch from hook, YO and pull up a loop, YO and draw through 2 loops on hook, YO, insert hook in same ch, YO and pull up a loop, YO and draw through 2 loops on hook, YO and draw through all 3 loops on hook.

SHELL
(2 Dc, ch 2, 2 dc) in sp indicated.

DECREASE (uses next 2 dc)
YO, † insert hook in next dc, YO and pull up a loop, YO and draw through 2 loops on hook †, YO, skip next joining, repeat from † to † once, YO and draw through all 3 loops on hook.

STRIP (Make 11)

CENTER

Foundation Row (Right side)**:** With White, ch 3, dc in third ch from hook (ring made), ★ work Cluster, ch 3, dc in third ch from hook; repeat from ★ 40 times **more**, ch 1; finish off: 41 Clusters and 42 rings.

Note: Loop a short piece of yarn around first Cluster worked to mark **right** side and **bottom** edge.

Rnd 1: With **right** side facing, join Teal with dc in last ring made ***(see Joining With Dc, page 68)***; (dc, ch 2, 2 dc, ch 3, work Shell) in same ring, ch 1, † skip next Cluster, ★ work Shell in next ring, ch 1, skip next Cluster; repeat from ★ across to last ring †, work (Shell, ch 3, Shell) in last ring, ch 1; working on opposite edge of Foundation Row, repeat from † to † once; join with slip st to first dc, finish off: 84 Shells.

Rnd 2: With **right** side facing, join White with dc in ch-3 sp at bottom edge of Strip; 2 dc in same sp, ch 1, † work Shell in next Shell (ch-2 sp), (tr in next ch-1 sp, work Shell in next Shell) across to next ch-3 sp, ch 1 †, (3 dc, ch 3, 3 dc) in ch-3 sp, ch 1, repeat from † to † once, 3 dc in same sp as first dc, dc in first dc to form last ch-3 sp.

Rnd 3: Ch 3 **(counts as first dc)**, (2 dc, ch 3, 3 dc) in last ch-3 sp made, † ch 1, (2 dc in next sp, ch 1) twice, place marker in last ch-1 made for joining, 2 dc in same sp, ch 2, (3 dc in next Shell, ch 2) across to last Shell on same side, 2 dc in last Shell, ch 1, place marker in last ch-1 made for joining, 2 dc in same sp, ch 1, 2 dc in next ch-1 sp, ch 1 †, (3 dc, ch 3, 3 dc) in next ch-3 sp, repeat from † to † once; join with slip st to first dc, finish off: 276 dc and 96 sps.

ASSEMBLY

Remove markers as Strips are joined leaving markers on outer Strips for Edging placement.

Holding two Strips together with bottom edges at the same end and using White, whipstitch Strips together ***(Fig. 5, page 69)***, beginning and ending in marked ch. Join remaining Strips in same manner.

EDGING

With **right** side facing, join White with sc in ch-1 sp after marked ch-1 on top edge ***(see Joining With Sc, page 68)***; † ch 1, (dc, ch 1) 3 times in next ch-1 sp, skip next 2 dc, sc in next dc, ch 1, (dc, ch 1) 3 times in next ch-3 sp, sc in next dc, ch 1, (dc, ch 1) 3 times in next ch-1 sp, sc in next ch-1 sp, ★ skip next dc, decrease, sc in next ch-1 sp, ch 1, (dc, ch 1) 3 times in next ch-1 sp, skip next 2 dc, sc in next dc, ch 1, (dc, ch 1) 3 times in next ch-3 sp, sc in next dc, ch 1, (dc, ch 1) 3 times in next ch-1 sp, sc in next ch-1 sp; repeat from ★ across to within 2 dc of next marker, ch 1, skip next 2 dc, (dc, ch 1) 3 times in marked sp, remove marker, sc in next ch-2 sp, [skip next dc, dc in next dc, (ch 1, dc in same st) twice, sc in next ch-2 sp] across to within 2 dc of next marker, ch 1, skip next 2 dc, (dc, ch 1) 3 times in marked sp, remove marker †, sc in next ch-1 sp, repeat from † to † once; join with slip st to first sc, finish off.

Tiny Twirls

Finished Size: 34¹/₂" x 45" (87.5 cm x 114.5 cm)

MATERIALS

Worsted Weight Yarn:
- Ecru - 23 ounces, 1,300 yards (650 grams, 1,188.5 meters)
- Purple - 3 ounces, 170 yards (90 grams, 155.5 meters)
- Pink - 3 ounces, 170 yards (90 grams, 155.5 meters)
- Yellow - 3 ounces, 170 yards (90 grams, 155.5 meters)
- Green - 3 ounces, 170 yards (90 grams, 155.5 meters)

Crochet hook, size I (5.5 mm) **or** size needed for gauge
Safety pin
Yarn needle

GAUGE SWATCH: 3¹/₂" (9 cm) square
Work same as Square.

STITCH GUIDE

TREBLE CROCHET *(abbreviated tr)*
YO twice, insert hook in st or sp indicated, YO and pull up a loop (4 loops on hook), (YO and draw through 2 loops on hook) 3 times.

FRONT POST TREBLE CROCHET *(abbreviated FPtr)*
YO twice, insert hook from **front** to **back** around post of dc indicated ***(Fig. A)***, YO and pull up a loop (4 loops on hook), (YO and draw through 2 loops on hook) 3 times. Skip st behind FPtr.

Fig. A

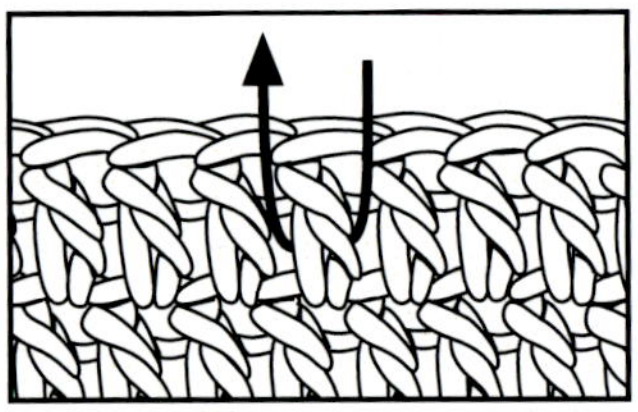

SQUARE (Make 108)

Working Rnd 3 with Purple, Pink, Yellow, or Green, make 27 Squares with **each** color.

Rnd 1 (Right side)**:** With Ecru, ch 2, 8 sc in second ch from hook; join with slip st to first sc.

Note: Loop a short piece of yarn around any stitch to mark Rnd 1 as **right** side.

Rnd 2: Ch 4 **(counts as first dc plus ch 1, now and throughout)**, dc in same st, ch 1, (dc, ch 1) twice in next sc and in each sc around; join with slip st to first dc; place loop from hook onto safety pin to keep piece from unraveling as you work the next rnd: 16 dc and 16 ch-1 sps.

Rnd 3: With **right** side facing and keeping safety pin and working yarn on **wrong** side of work, join color indicated with slip st around post of last dc made ***(Fig. A)***; ch 5 **(counts as first FPtr plus ch 1)**, work FPtr around next dc, place marker around last ch made for st placement, ch 1, (FPtr around next dc, ch 1) around; join with slip st to first FPtr, finish off.

Rnd 4: With **right** side facing, remove safety pin and place Ecru loop onto hook, ch 1, working **behind** sts on Rnd 3 ***(Fig. 4, page 69)***, sc in next ch-1 sp on Rnd 2, sc in marked sp on Rnd 3, remove marker, (sc in next ch-1 sp on Rnd 2, sc in next ch-1 sp on Rnd 3) around; join with slip st to first sc: 32 sc.

Continued on page 54.

Rnd 5: Ch 4, ★ † skip next sc, sc in next sc, ch 1, skip next sc, slip st in next sc, ch 1, skip next sc, sc in next sc, ch 1, skip next sc †, (dc, ch 3, dc) in next sc, ch 1; repeat from ★ 2 times **more**, then repeat from † to † once, dc in same st as first dc, ch 3; join with slip st to first dc, finish off: 20 sts and 20 sps.

ASSEMBLY

With Ecru and using Placement Diagram as a guide, whipstitch Squares together forming 9 vertical strips of 12 Squares each ***(Fig. 5, page 69)***, beginning in center ch of first corner ch-3 and ending in center ch of next corner ch-3; then whipstitch strips together in same manner.

PLACEMENT DIAGRAM

A	B	A	B	A	B	A	B	A
C	D	C	D	C	D	C	D	C
B	A	B	A	B	A	B	A	B
D	C	D	C	D	C	D	C	D
A	B	A	B	A	B	A	B	A
C	D	C	D	C	D	C	D	C
B	A	B	A	B	A	B	A	B
D	C	D	C	D	C	D	C	D
A	B	A	B	A	B	A	B	A
C	D	C	D	C	D	C	D	C
B	A	B	A	B	A	B	A	B
D	C	D	C	D	C	D	C	D

KEY

A - Purple

B - Pink

C - Yellow

D - Green

EDGING

Rnd 1: With **right** side facing, join Ecru with sc in any corner ch-3 sp ***(see Joining With Sc, page 68)***; ch 3, sc in same sp, ch 1, (sc in next sp, ch 1) across to next corner ch-3 sp, ★ (sc, ch 3, sc) in corner ch-3 sp, ch 1, (sc in next sp, ch 1) across to next corner ch-3 sp; repeat from ★ 2 times **more**; join with slip st to first sc: 252 sc and 252 sps.

Rnd 2: Ch 1, turn; ★ (sc in next ch-1 sp, ch 1) across to next corner ch-3 sp, (sc, ch 3, sc) in corner ch-3 sp, ch 1; repeat from ★ around; join with slip st to first sc, finish off: 260 sc and 260 sps.

Rnd 3: With **right** side facing, working in **front** of Rnd 2 and in sc and corner ch-3 sps on Rnd 1, join Pink with slip st in first corner ch-3 sp (between sc); ch 5, † (tr in next sc, ch 1) across to next corner ch-3 sp, tr in corner ch-3 sp †, ch 2, cut Pink; with Yellow, ch 1, tr in same sp, ch 1; repeat from † to † once, ch 2, cut Yellow; with Green, ch 1, tr in same sp, ch 1; repeat from † to † once, ch 2, cut Green; with Purple, ch 1, tr in same sp, ch 1; repeat from † to † once, ch 3; join with slip st to first tr, finish off.

Rnd 4: With **right** side facing, join Ecru with sc in any corner ch-3 sp; working **behind** Rnd 3, sc in ch-1 sp after corner ch-3 sp on Rnd 2, ★ † sc in same corner ch-3 sp on Rnd 3, (sc in next ch-1 sp on Rnd 2, sc in next ch-1 sp on Rnd 3) across to within 2 ch-1 sps of next corner ch-3 sp on Rnd 3, sc in next corner ch-3 sp on Rnd 2, sc in next ch-1 sp on Rnd 3, sc in same corner ch-3 sp on Rnd 2, sc in next ch-1 sp on Rnd 3, place marker in last sc made for st placement, sc in same corner ch-3 sp on Rnd 2 †, sc in next corner ch-3 sp on Rnd 3, sc in next ch-1 sp on Rnd 2; repeat from ★ 2 times **more**, then repeat from † to † once; join with slip st to first sc.

Rnd 5: Ch 1, sc in same st, ch 1, skip next sc, ★ (sc in next sc, ch 1, skip next sc) across to marked sc, (sc, ch 1) twice in marked sc, remove marker, skip next sc; repeat from ★ 3 times **more**, sc in next sc, ch 1; join with slip st to first sc.

Rnd 6: (Slip st in next ch-1 sp, ch 1) around; join with slip st to first slip st, finish off.

Universal Appeal

Finished Size: 48" x 66" (122 cm x 167.5 cm)

MATERIALS

Worsted Weight Yarn:
- Black - 42 ounces, 2,375 yards (1,190 grams, 2,171.5 meters)
- Scraps - 14 ounces, 790 yards (400 grams, 722.5 meters) **total**

Crochet hook, size I (5.5 mm) **or** size needed for gauge

Yarn needle

GAUGE: Each Motif = 4 1/2" (11.5 cm) (straight edge to straight edge)

Gauge Swatch: 3 1/2" (9 cm) diameter
Work same as Motif through Rnd 2.

STITCH GUIDE

TREBLE CROCHET *(abbreviated tr)*
YO twice, insert hook in stitch indicated, YO and pull up a loop (4 loops on hook), (YO and draw through 2 loops on hook) 3 times.

CHANGING COLORS

Work the last dc to within one step of completion (2 loops on hook), hook new yarn ***(Fig. A)*** and draw through both loops on hook. Work **over** color not being used; cut yarn at end of rnd.

Fig. A

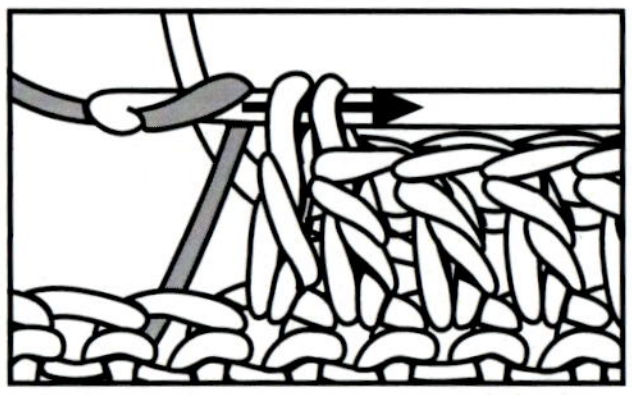

MOTIF (Make 140)

With Black, ch 6; join with slip st to form a ring.

Rnd 1 (Right side)**:** Ch 3 **(counts as first dc, now and throughout)**, 15 dc in ring; join with slip st to first dc, finish off: 16 dc.

Note: Loop a short piece of yarn around any stitch to mark Rnd 1 as **right** side.

Rnd 2: With **right** side facing, join first scrap color with dc in any dc ***(see Joining With Dc, page 68)***; dc in same st, 2 dc in next dc changing to second scrap color in last dc made ***(Fig. A)***, (2 dc in each of next 2 dc changing colors in last dc made) around; join with slip st to first dc, finish off: 32 dc.

Rnd 3: With **right** side facing, join Black with dc in same st as joining; dc in next dc, 2 dc in next dc, dc in next dc, ch 1, ★ dc in next 2 dc, 2 dc in next dc, dc in next dc, ch 1; repeat from ★ around; join with slip st to first dc, finish off: 40 dc and 8 ch-1 sps.

FILL-IN MOTIF (Make 117)

With Black, ch 6; join with slip st to form a ring.

Rnd 1 (Right side)**:** Ch 3, 2 dc in ring, ch 3, (3 dc in ring, ch 3) 3 times; join with slip st to first dc, finish off: 12 dc and 4 ch-3 sps.

Note: Mark Rnd 1 as **right** side.

TRIANGLE (Make 44)

Row 1 (Right side)**:** With Black, ch 6; (3 dc, ch 3, 3 dc, ch 1, tr) in sixth ch from hook **(5 skipped chs count as first tr plus ch 1)**; finish off: 8 sts and 3 sps.

Note: Mark Row 1 as **right** side.

ASSEMBLY

With Black and using Placement Diagram as a guide, whipstitch Motifs together forming 10 vertical strips of 14 Motifs each ***(Fig. 5, page 69)***, beginning in first corner ch and ending in next corner ch; then whipstitch strips together in same manner.

Using Placement Diagram as a guide, whipstitch Fill-In Motifs to Motifs in same manner, matching center ch of corner ch-3 on Fill-In Motif to joined chs on Motifs; whipstitch Triangles to Motifs, matching center ch of ch-3 on Triangle to joined ch on Motif and tr to unjoined ch on Motifs.

PLACEMENT DIAGRAM

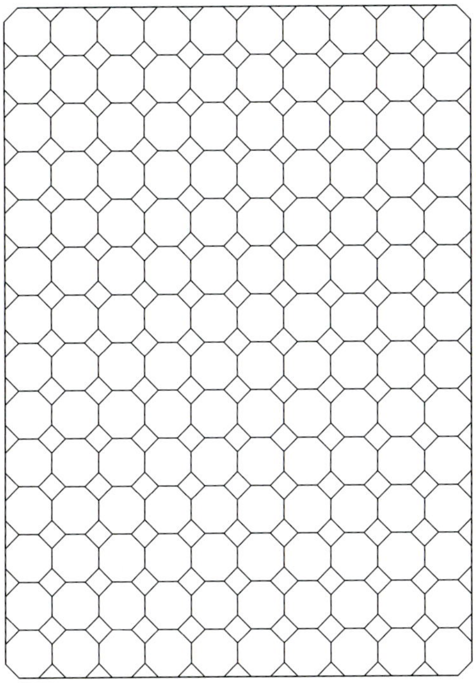

EDGING

Rnd 1: With **right** side facing and working across short edge of Afghan, join Black with dc in second corner ch-1 sp on corner Motif; ch 1, dc in same sp, dc in next 5 dc, ★ † [ch 1, (sc, ch 1) twice around post of each of next 2 tr on Triangle, dc in next 5 dc on Motif] across to next corner ch-1 sp †, [(dc, ch 1, dc) in next corner ch-1 sp, dc in next 5 dc] twice; repeat from ★ 2 times **more**, then repeat from † to † once, (dc, ch 1, dc) in corner ch-1 sp, dc in next 5 dc; join with slip st to first dc: 452 sts and 228 ch-1 sps.

Rnd 2: (Slip st, ch 4, dc) in next corner ch-1 sp, ★ † dc in next 6 dc and in next ch-1 sp, (dc in next sc and in next ch-1 sp) 4 times, [dc in next 5 dc and in next ch-1 sp, (dc in next sc and in next ch-1 sp) 4 times] across to within 6 dc of next corner ch-1 sp, dc in next 6 dc, (dc, ch 1, dc) in next corner ch-1 sp, dc in next 7 dc †, (dc, ch 1, dc) in next corner ch-1 sp; repeat from ★ 2 times **more**, then repeat from † to † once; join with slip st to third ch of beginning ch-4: 688 sts and 8 ch-1 sps.

Rnd 3: (Slip st, ch 1, sc) in next corner ch-1 sp, ch 1, sc in next dc, (ch 1, skip next dc, sc in next dc) across to next corner ch-1 sp, ch 1, ★ sc in corner ch-1 sp, ch 1, sc in next dc, (ch 1, skip next dc, sc in next dc) across to next corner ch-1 sp, ch 1; repeat from ★ around; join with slip st to first sc.

Rnd 4: (Slip st in next ch-1 sp, ch 1) around; join with slip st to first slip st, finish off.

Vision in Black

Finished Size: 48" x $64^1/_2$" (122 cm x 164 cm)

MATERIALS

Worsted Weight Yarn:
 Variegated - 36 ounces, 2,090 yards (1,020 grams, 1,911 meters)
 Black - 33 ounces, 1,865 yards (940 grams, 1,705.5 meters)
Crochet hook, size I (5.5 mm) **or** size needed for gauge

GAUGE: In pattern,
16 sts and 16 rows = $4^1/_2$" (11.5 cm)

Gauge Swatch: 6"w x $4^1/_2$"h (15 cm x 11.5 cm)
With Variegated, ch 22.
Work same as Afghan Body for 16 rows.

Each row is worked across length of Afghan. When joining yarn and finishing off, leave an 8" (20.5 cm) end to be worked into fringe.

STITCH GUIDE

ANCHOR DC
YO, insert hook in st indicated **and** in back ridge of fourth ch of ch-7 ***(Fig. A)***, YO and pull up a loop, (YO and draw through 2 loops on hook) twice.

Fig. A

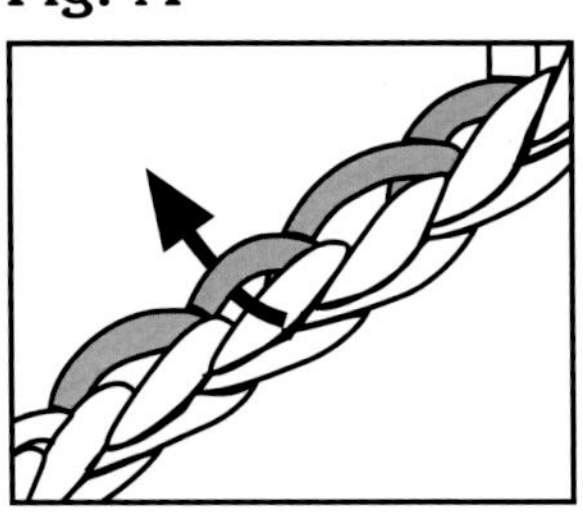

AFGHAN BODY

With Variegated, ch 230.

Row 1 (Wrong side)**:** Sc in second ch from hook and in each ch across; finish off: 229 sc.

Note: Loop a short piece of yarn around the **back** of any stitch on Row 1 to mark **right** side.

Row 2 (Right side)**:** With **right** side facing, join Black with sc in first sc ***(see Joining With Sc, page 68)***; ★ ch 1, skip next sc, sc in next sc; repeat from ★ across; finish off: 115 sc and 114 ch-1 sps.

Row 3: With **wrong** side facing, join Variegated with sc in first sc; ★ working **behind** next ch-1 ***(Fig. 4, page 69)***, dc in skipped sc one row **below**, sc in next sc on Row 2; repeat from ★ across, finish off: 229 sts.

Row 4: With **right** side facing, join Black with sc in first sc; ch 1, skip next dc, sc in next sc, ch 1, ★ skip next dc, sc in next 5 sts, ch 1, skip next dc, sc in next sc, ch 1; repeat from ★ across to last 2 sts, skip next dc, sc in last sc; finish off: 171 sc and 58 ch-1 sps.

Row 5: With **wrong** side facing, join Variegated with sc in first sc; working **behind** next ch-1, dc in skipped dc one row **below**, sc in next sc on Row 4, working **behind** next ch-1, dc in skipped dc one row **below**, ★ ch 7, working **behind** next ch-1, dc in skipped dc one row **below**, sc in next sc on Row 4, working **behind** next ch-1, dc in skipped dc one row **below**; repeat from ★ across to last sc on Row 4, sc in last sc; finish off: 89 sts and 28 ch-7 sps.

Row 6: With **right** side facing, join Black with sc in first sc; ch 1, skip next dc, sc in next sc, ch 1, ★ skip next dc, working in **front** of next ch-7, dc in next 2 skipped sts one row **below**, work Anchor Dc in next st one row **below**, dc in next 2 skipped sts one row **below**, ch 1, skip next dc, sc in next sc, ch 1; repeat from ★ across to last 2 sts, skip next dc, sc in last sc; finish off: 171 sc and 58 ch-1 sps.

Rows 7 and 8: Repeat Rows 5 and 6.

Row 9: With **wrong** side facing, join Variegated with sc in first sc; working **behind** next ch-1, dc in skipped dc one row **below**, sc in next sc on Row 8, working **behind** next ch-1, dc in skipped dc one row **below**, ★ sc in next 5 dc on Row 8, working **behind** next ch-1, dc in skipped dc one row **below**, sc in next sc on Row 8, working **behind** next ch-1, dc in skipped dc one row **below**; repeat from ★ across to last sc, sc in last sc; finish off: 229 sts.

Row 10: With **right** side facing, join Black with sc in first sc; ★ ch 1, skip next st, sc in next sc; repeat from ★ across; finish off: 115 sc and 114 ch-1 sps.

Row 11: With **wrong** side facing, join Variegated with sc in first sc; ★ working **behind** next ch-1, dc in skipped st one row **below**, sc in next sc on Row 10; repeat from ★ across; finish off: 229 sts.

Rows 12-171: Repeat Rows 4-11, 20 times.

TRIM

FIRST SIDE

With **right** side facing, join Variegated with slip st in first sc on Row 171; ★ ch 1, skip next dc, slip st in next sc; repeat from ★ across; finish off.

SECOND SIDE

With **right** side facing and working in free loops of beginning ch ***(Fig. 2, page 69)***, join Variegated with slip st in ch at base of first sc; ★ ch 1, skip next ch, slip st in next ch; repeat from ★ across; finish off.

Holding 2 strands of corresponding color yarn together, each 17" (43 cm) long, add additional fringe in each row across short edges of Afghan ***(Figs. 6a & b, page 69)***.

Wonderfully Original

Finished Size: 49" x 65" (124.5 cm x 165 cm)

MATERIALS

Worsted Weight Yarn:
- Lt Blue - 17 ounces, 960 yards (480 grams, 878 meters)
- Blue - 17 ounces, 960 yards (480 grams, 878 meters)
- Tan - 16 ounces, 905 yards (450 grams, 827.5 meters)
- Brown - 16 ounces, 905 yards (450 grams, 827.5 meters)

Crochet hook, size I (5.5 mm) **or** size needed for gauge

GAUGE: In pattern, (sc, ch 6) 3 times and 12 rows = $3^1/_2$" (9 cm)

Gauge Swatch: $3^3/_4$" (9.5 cm) square
With Lt Blue, ch 14.
Rows 1-9: Work same as Afghan Body.
Row 10: Work Last Row.

Each row is worked across length of Afghan. When joining yarn and finishing off, leave a 9" (23 cm) end to be worked into fringe.

AFGHAN BODY

With Lt Blue, ch 222.

Row 1 (Right side)**:** Sc in second ch from hook, ★ ch 1, skip next ch, sc in next ch; repeat from ★ across; finish off: 111 sc and 110 ch-1 sps.

Note: Loop a short piece of yarn around any stitch to mark Row 1 as **right** side.

Row 2: With **wrong** side facing, join Blue with sc in first sc ***(see Joining With Sc, page 68)***; ★ ch 6, skip next sc, sc in next sc; repeat from ★ across; finish off: 56 sc and 55 ch-6 sps.

Row 3: With **right** side facing, join Tan with sc in first sc; ch 2, working **behind** next ch-6 ***(Fig. 4, page 69)***, sc in skipped sc on Row 1, ★ ch 6, working in **front** of next ch-6, sc in next skipped sc on Row 1, ch 6, working **behind** next ch-6, sc in next skipped sc on Row 1; repeat from ★ across to last sc on Row 2, ch 2, sc in last sc; finish off: 57 sc and 56 sps.

Row 4: With **wrong** side facing, join Brown with sc in first sc; ch 6, (sc in next ch-6 sp, ch 6) across, sc in last sc; finish off: 56 sc and 55 ch-6 sps.

Row 5: With **right** side facing, join Lt Blue with sc in first sc; ch 2, working in **front** of next ch-6, sc in next ch-6 sp two rows **below**, ★ ch 6, working **behind** next ch-6, sc in next ch-6 sp two rows **below**, ch 6, working in **front** of next ch-6, sc in next ch-6 sp two rows **below**; repeat from ★ across to last sc on Row 4, ch 2, sc in last sc; finish off: 57 sc and 56 sps.

Row 6: With **wrong** side facing, join Blue with sc in first sc; ch 6, (sc in next ch-6 sp, ch 6) across, sc in last sc; finish off: 56 sc and 55 ch-6 sps.

Row 7: With **right** side facing, join Tan with sc in first sc; ch 2, working **behind** next ch-6, sc in next ch-6 sp two rows **below**, ★ ch 6, working in **front** of next ch-6, sc in next ch-6 sp two rows **below**, ch 6, working **behind** next ch-6, sc in next ch-6 sp two rows **below**; repeat from ★ across to last sc, ch 2, sc in last sc on Row 6; finish off: 57 sc and 56 sps.

Row 8: With **wrong** side facing, join Brown with sc in first sc; ch 6, (sc in next ch-6 sp, ch 6) across, sc in last sc; finish off: 56 sc and 55 ch-6 sps.

Row 9: With **right** side facing, join Lt Blue with sc in first sc; ch 2, working in **front** of next ch-6, sc in next ch-6 sp two rows **below**, ★ ch 6, working **behind** next ch-6, sc in next ch-6 sp two rows **below**, ch 6, working in **front** of next ch-6, sc in next ch-6 sp two rows **below**; repeat from ★ across to last sc, ch 2, sc in last sc on Row 8; finish off: 57 sc and 56 sps.

Repeat Rows 6-9 for pattern until Afghan Body measures approximately $48^1/_2$" (123 cm) from beginning ch, ending by working Row 9.

Last Row: With **wrong** side facing, join Lt Blue with sc in first sc; ch 1, sc in next ch-6 sp one row **below**, ch 1, ★ sc in next ch-6 sp on previous row, ch 1, sc in next ch-6 sp one row **below**, ch 1; repeat from ★ across, sc in last sc; finish off.

TRIM

FIRST SIDE

With **right** side facing, join Lt Blue with slip st in first sc on Last Row; slip st in next ch-1 sp, (ch 1, slip st in next ch-1 sp) across, slip st in last sc; finish off.

SECOND SIDE

With **right** side facing and working in sps and in free loops of beginning ch ***(Fig. 2, page 69)***, join Lt Blue with slip st in first ch; slip st in next sp, (ch 1, slip st in next sp) across to ch at base of last sc, slip st in ch at base of last sc; finish off.

Holding 2 strands **each** of Lt Blue and Blue together, each 19" (48.5 cm) long, add additional fringe evenly spaced across short edges of Afghan ***(Figs. 6a & b, page 69)***.

Xtra Easy

Finished Size: 48" x 64" (122 cm x 162.5 cm)

MATERIALS

Worsted Weight Yarn:
- Black - 21 ounces, 1,185 yards (600 grams, 1,083.5 meters)
- Off-White - 12 ounces, 680 yards (340 grams, 622 meters)
- Burgundy - 8 ounces, 450 yards (230 grams, 411.5 meters)
- Green - 8 ounces, 450 yards (230 grams, 411.5 meters)
- Yellow - 8 ounces, 450 yards (230 grams, 411.5 meters)

Crochet hook, size I (5.5 mm) **or** size needed for gauge

GAUGE: In pattern, (sc, ch 1) 11 times and 22 rows = 6" (15.25 cm)

Gauge Swatch: 3" (7.5 cm) square
With Black, ch 12.
Work same as Afghan Body for 11 rows.

Each row is worked across length of Afghan. When joining yarn and finishing off, leave an 8" (20.5 cm) end to be worked into fringe.

AFGHAN BODY

With Black, ch 236.

Row 1 (Right side)**:** Sc in second ch from hook and in next ch, ch 1, ★ skip next ch, sc in next ch, ch 1; repeat from ★ across to last 3 chs, skip next ch, sc in last 2 chs; finish off: 119 sc and 116 ch-1 sps.

Note: Loop a short piece of yarn around any stitch to mark Row 1 as **right** side.

Row 2: With **wrong** side facing, join Black with sc in first sc ***(see Joining With Sc, page 68)***; ch 1, ★ skip next sc, sc in next ch-1 sp, ch 1; repeat from ★ across to last 2 sc, skip next sc, sc in last sc; finish off: 118 sc and 117 ch-1 sps.

Row 3: With **right** side facing, join Off-White with sc in first sc; sc in next ch-1 sp, ★ ch 1, skip next sc, sc in next ch-1 sp; repeat from ★ across to last sc, sc in last sc; finish off: 119 sc and 116 ch-1 sps.

Rows 4 and 5: Repeat Rows 2 and 3.

Rows 6 and 7: With Black, repeat Rows 2 and 3.

Row 8: With Burgundy, repeat Row 2.

Row 9: With Green, repeat Row 3.

Row 10: With Yellow, repeat Row 2.

Row 11: Repeat Row 3.

Row 12: With Yellow, repeat Row 2.

Row 13: With Green, repeat Row 3.

Row 14: With Burgundy, repeat Row 2.

Row 15: With Black, repeat Row 3.

Rows 16-175: Repeat Rows 2-15, 11 times; then repeat Rows 2-7 once **more**.

TRIM

FIRST SIDE

With **right** side facing, join Black with slip st in first sc; ch 1, ★ skip next sc, slip st in next ch-1 sp, ch 1; repeat from ★ across to last 2 sc, skip next sc, slip st in last sc; finish off.

SECOND SIDE

With **right** side facing and working in sps and in free loops of beginning ch ***(Fig. 2, page 69)***, join Black with slip st in first ch; ch 1, skip next ch, ★ slip st in next sp, ch 1, skip next ch; repeat from ★ across to ch at base of last sc, slip st in ch at base of last sc; finish off.

Holding 2 strands of corresponding color yarn together, each 17" (43 cm) long, add additional fringe evenly spaced across short edges of Afghan ***(Figs. 6a & b, page 69)***.

Yen for Yo-Yos

Finished Size: 48" x $64^1/2$" (122 cm x 164 cm)

MATERIALS

Worsted Weight Yarn:
Black - 30 ounces, 1,695 yards (850 grams, 1,550 meters)
Scrap Colors - 29 ounces, 1,640 yards (820 grams, 1,499.5 meters) **total**
Crochet hook, size I (5.5 mm) **or** size needed for gauge
Yarn needle

GAUGE: Each Square = $3^1/4$" (8.25 cm)

Gauge Swatch: $2^1/2$" (6.25 cm) diameter
Work same as Square through Rnd 2.

SQUARE (Make 234)

With Scrap color, ch 5; join with slip st to form a ring.

Rnd 1 (Right side): Ch 3 **(counts as first dc)**, 15 dc in ring; join with slip st to first dc, finish off: 16 dc.

Note: Loop a short piece of yarn around any stitch to mark Rnd 1 as **right** side.

Rnd 2: With **wrong** side facing, join Scrap color with sc in same st as joining ***(see Joining With Sc, page 68)***; ch 1, (sc in next dc, ch 1) around; join with slip st to first sc, finish off: 16 sc and 16 ch-1 sps.

Rnd 3: With **right** side facing, join Black with sc in any sc; ch 1, (sc in next sc, ch 1) around; join with slip st to first sc, do **not** finish off.

Rnd 4: Ch 1, sc in same st, ch 1, (dc, ch 3, dc) in next sc, ch 1, sc in next sc, ch 1, slip st in next sc, ch 1, ★ sc in next sc, ch 1, (dc, ch 3, dc) in next sc, ch 1, sc in next sc, ch 1, slip st in next sc, ch 1; repeat from ★ 2 times **more**; join with slip st to first sc, finish off: 20 sts and 20 sps.

ASSEMBLY

With Black, whipstitch Squares together forming 13 vertical strips of 18 Squares each ***(Fig. 5, page 69)***, beginning in center ch of first corner ch-3 and ending in center ch of next corner ch-3; then whipstitch strips together in same manner.

EDGING

Rnd 1: With **right** side facing, join Black with sc in any corner ch-3 sp; ch 2, sc in same sp, ch 1, (sc in next sp, ch 1) across to next corner ch-3 sp, ★ (sc, ch 2, sc) in corner ch-3 sp, ch 1, (sc in next sp, ch 1) across to next corner ch-3 sp; repeat from ★ 2 times **more**; join with slip st to first sc: 372 sc and 372 sps.

Rnd 2: Ch 1, turn; ★ (sc in next ch-1 sp, ch 1) across to next corner ch-2 sp, (sc, ch 2, sc) in corner ch-2 sp, ch 1; repeat from ★ around; join with slip st to first sc, finish off: 376 sc and 376 sps.

Rnd 3: With **right** side facing, join Scrap color with sc in any corner ch-2 sp; ch 2, sc in same sp, ch 1, (sc in next ch-1 sp, ch 1) across to next corner ch-2 sp, ★ (sc, ch 2, sc) in corner ch-2 sp, ch 1, (sc in next ch-1 sp, ch 1) across to next corner ch-2 sp; repeat from ★ 2 times **more**; join with slip st to first sc, finish off: 380 sc and 380 sps.

Rnd 4: With **wrong** side facing, join Scrap color with sc in any corner ch-2 sp; ch 2, sc in same sp, ch 1, (sc in next ch-1 sp, ch 1) across to next corner ch-2 sp, ★ (sc, ch 2, sc) in corner ch-2 sp, ch 1, (sc in next ch-1 sp, ch 1) across to next corner ch-2 sp; repeat from ★ 2 times **more**; join with slip st to first sc, finish off: 384 sc and 384 sps.

Rnds 5-10: With Scrap color, repeat Rnds 3 and 4, 3 times: 408 sc and 408 sps.

Rnd 11: With Black, repeat Rnd 3; do **not** finish off.

Rnd 12: ★ (Slip st, ch 2, slip st) in next corner ch-2 sp, ch 1, (slip st in next ch-1 sp, ch 1) across to next corner ch-2 sp; repeat from ★ around; join with slip st to first slip st, finish off.

Zeal for Zig-Zags

Finished Size: 50" x $67^1/_2$"
(127 cm x 171.5 cm)

MATERIALS

Worsted Weight Yarn:
- Black - 17 ounces, 1,165 yards (480 grams, 1,065.5 meters)
- Rose - 15 ounces, 1,030 yards (430 grams, 942 meters)
- Brown - 13 ounces, 890 yards (370 grams, 814 meters)
- Tan - 13 ounces, 890 yards (370 grams, 814 meters)
- Green - $7^1/_2$ ounces, 515 yards (210 grams, 471 meters)
- Peach - $6^1/_2$ ounces, 445 yards (180 grams, 407 meters)

Crochet hook, size I (5.5 mm) **or** size needed for gauge

GAUGE: In pattern,
one repeat = $2^1/_2$" (6.25 cm);
8 rows = 3" (7.5 cm)

Gauge Swatch: 5"w x 3"h (12.75 cm x 7.5 cm)
With Black, ch 24.
Work same as Afghan for 8 rows.

Each row is worked across length of Afghan. When joining yarn and finishing off, leave an 8" (20.5 cm) end to be worked into fringe.

AFGHAN BODY

With Black, ch 324.

Row 1 (Right side)**:** Sc in second ch from hook and in next 4 chs, 3 sc in next ch, sc in next 5 chs, ★ skip next ch, sc in next 5 chs, 3 sc in next ch, sc in next 5 chs; repeat from ★ across; finish off: 351 sc.

Note: Loop a short piece of yarn around any stitch to mark Row 1 as **right** side.

Row 2: With **wrong** side facing and working in Back Loops Only ***(Fig. 1, page 68)***, join Black with sc in first sc ***(see Joining With Sc, page 68)***; skip next sc, sc in next 4 sc, 3 sc in next sc, ★ sc in next 5 sc, skip next 2 sc, sc in next 5 sc, 3 sc in next sc; repeat from ★ across to last 6 sc, sc in next 4 sc, skip next sc, sc in last sc; finish off.

Row 3: With **right** side facing and working in Back Loops Only, join Rose with sc in first sc; skip next sc, sc in next 4 sc, 3 sc in next sc, ★ sc in next 5 sc, skip next 2 sc, sc in next 5 sc, 3 sc in next sc; repeat from ★ across to last 6 sc, sc in next 4 sc, skip next sc, sc in last sc; finish off.

Row 4: With **wrong** side facing and working in Back Loops Only, join Rose with sc in first sc; skip next sc, sc in next 4 sc, 3 sc in next sc, ★ sc in next 5 sc, skip next 2 sc, sc in next 5 sc, 3 sc in next sc; repeat from ★ across to last 6 sc, sc in next 4 sc, skip next sc, sc in last sc; finish off.

Rows 5 and 6: With Green, repeat Rows 3 and 4.

Rows 7 and 8: Repeat Rows 3 and 4.

Rows 9 and 10: With Black, repeat Rows 3 and 4.

Rows 11 and 12: With Brown, repeat Rows 3 and 4.

Rows 13 and 14: With Tan, repeat Rows 3 and 4.

Rows 15 and 16: With Peach, repeat Rows 3 and 4.

Rows 17 and 18: With Tan, repeat Rows 3 and 4.

Rows 19 and 20: With Brown, repeat Rows 3 and 4.

Rows 21 and 22: With Black, repeat Rows 3 and 4.

Rows 23-130: Repeat Rows 3-22, 5 times; then repeat Rows 3-10 once **more**.

TRIM

FIRST SIDE

With **right** side facing and working in both loops, join Black with slip st in first sc on Row 130; ch 2, (skip next sc, slip st in next sc, ch 2) twice, skip next sc, (slip st, ch 2, slip st) in next sc, ★ ch 2, (skip next sc, slip st in next sc, ch 2) twice, skip next sc, slip st in next 2 sc, ch 2, (skip next sc, slip st in next sc, ch 2) twice, skip next sc, (slip st, ch 2, slip st) in

SECOND SIDE

With **right** side facing and working in free loops of beginning ch ***(Fig. 2, page 69)***, join Black with slip st in first ch; slip st in next ch, ch 2, skip next ch, slip st in next ch, (ch 1, skip next ch, slip st in next ch) twice, ★ ch 2, skip next ch, slip st in next ch, ch 2, skip next ch, (slip st, ch 2, slip st) in next sp, (ch 2, skip next ch, slip st in next ch) twice, (ch 1, skip next ch, slip st in next ch) twice; repeat from ★ across to last 3 chs, ch 2, skip next ch, slip st in last 2 chs; finish off.

Holding 2 strands of corresponding color together, each 17" (43 cm) long, add additional fringe in each row across short edges of Afghan ***(Figs. 6a & b, page 69)***.

GENERAL INSTRUCTIONS

ABBREVIATIONS

ch(s) chain(s)
cm centimeters
dc double crochet(s)
FPtr Front Post treble crochet(s)
hdc half double crochet(s)
mm millimeters
Rnd(s) Round(s)
sc single crochet(s)
sp(s) space(s)
st(s) stitch(es)
tr treble crochet(s)
YO yarn over

★ — work instructions following ★ as many **more** times as indicated in addition to the first time.

† to † — work all instructions from first † to second † **as many** times as specified.

( ) or **[ ]** — work enclosed instructions **as many** times as specified by the number immediately following **or** work all enclosed instructions in the stitch or space indicated **or** contains explanatory remarks.

colon (:) — the number(s) given after a colon at the end of a row or round denote(s) the number of stitches or spaces you should have on that row or round.

CROCHET TERMINOLOGY	
UNITED STATES	**INTERNATIONAL**
slip stitch (slip st) =	single crochet (sc)
single crochet (sc) =	double crochet (dc)
half double crochet (hdc) =	half treble crochet (htr)
double crochet (dc) =	treble crochet (tr)
treble crochet (tr) =	double treble crochet (dtr)
double treble crochet (dtr) =	triple treble crochet (ttr)
triple treble crochet (tr tr) =	quadruple treble crochet (qtr)
skip =	miss

GAUGE

Exact gauge is **essential** for proper size. Before beginning your Afghan, make the sample swatch given in the individual instructions in the yarn and hook specified. After completing the swatch, measure it, counting your stitches and rows or rounds carefully. If your swatch is larger or smaller than specified, **make another, changing hook size to get the correct gauge**. Keep trying until you find the size hook that will give you the specified gauge.

JOINING WITH SC

When instructed to join with sc, begin with a slip knot on hook. Insert hook in stitch or space indicated, YO and pull up a loop, YO and draw through both loops on hook.

JOINING WITH DC

When instructed to join with dc, begin with a slip knot on hook. YO, holding loop on hook, insert hook in stitch or space indicated, YO and pull up a loop (3 loops on hook), (YO and draw through 2 loops on hook) twice.

BACK LOOP ONLY

Work only in loop(s) indicated by arrow ***(Fig. 1)***.

Fig. 1

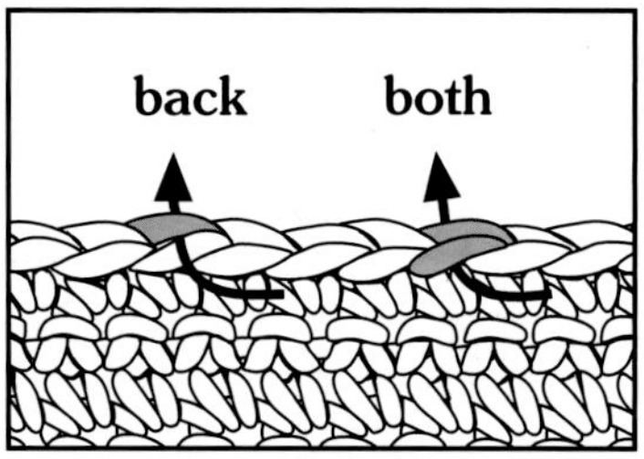

ALUMINUM CROCHET HOOKS													
U.S.	B-1	C-2	D-3	E-4	F-5	G-6	H-8	I-9	J-10	K-10½	N	P	Q
Metric - mm	2.25	2.75	3.25	3.5	3.75	4	5	5.5	6	6.5	9	10	15

FREE LOOPS OF A CHAIN

When instructed to work in free loops of a chain, work in loop indicated by arrow ***(Fig. 2)***.

Fig. 2

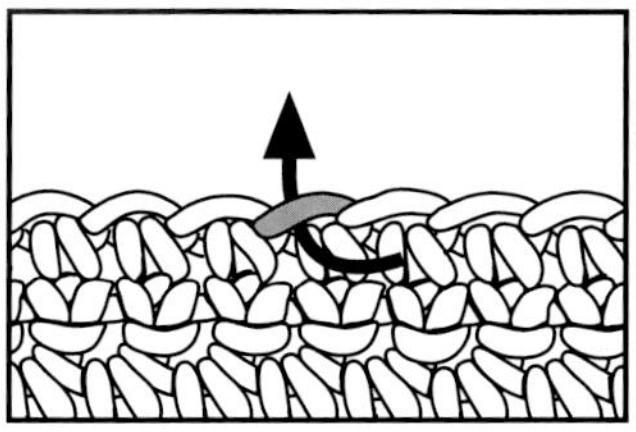

WORKING IN TOP 2 LOOPS OF A CHAIN

Work only in loops indicated by arrow ***(Fig. 3)***.

Fig. 3

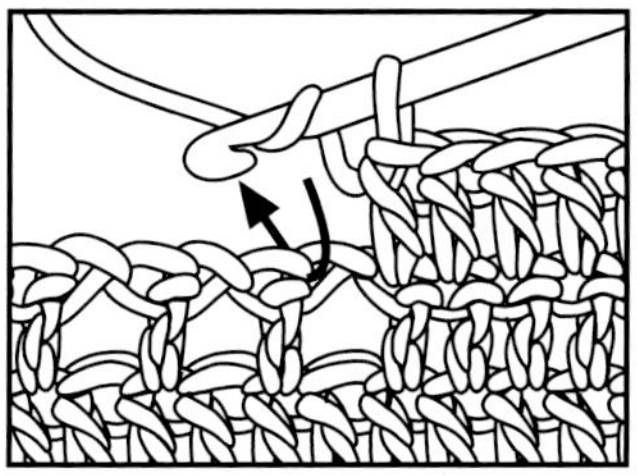

WORKING IN FRONT OF, AROUND, OR BEHIND A STITCH

Work in stitch or space indicated, inserting hook in direction of arrow ***(Fig. 4)***.

Fig. 4

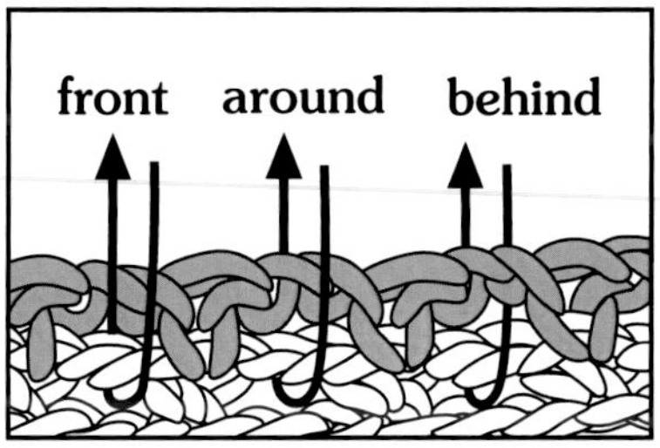

WHIPSTITCH

Place two Squares, Strips, or Motifs with **wrong** sides together. Sew through both pieces once to secure the beginning of the seam, leaving an ample yarn end to weave in later. Working through **both** loops on **both** pieces, insert needle from **front** to **back** through first stitch and pull yarn through ***(Fig. 5)***. ★ Insert the needle from **front** to **back** through next stitch on both pieces and pull yarn through; repeat from ★ across.
Repeat along the edge, being careful to match stitches and rows.

Fig. 5

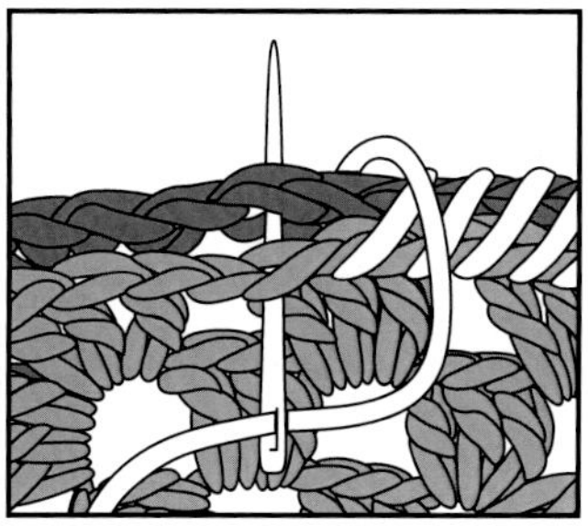

FRINGE

Cut a piece of cardboard 8" (20.5 cm) wide and half as long as strands indicated in individual instructions. Wind the yarn **loosely** and **evenly** lengthwise around the cardboard until the card is filled, then cut across one end; repeat as needed.
Hold together as many strands of yarn as specified in the individual instructions; fold in half.
With **wrong** side facing and using a crochet hook, draw the folded end up through a row and pull the loose ends through the folded end ***(Fig. 6a)***; draw the knot up **tightly** ***(Fig. 6b)***. Repeat, spacing as specified in individual instructions.
Lay flat on a hard surface and trim the ends.

Fig. 6a

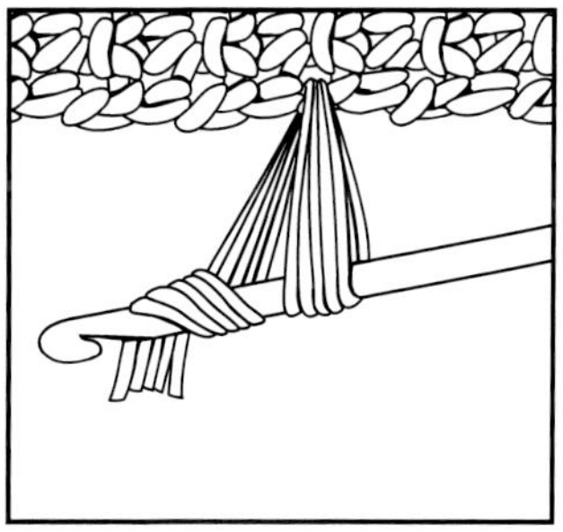

Fig. 6b

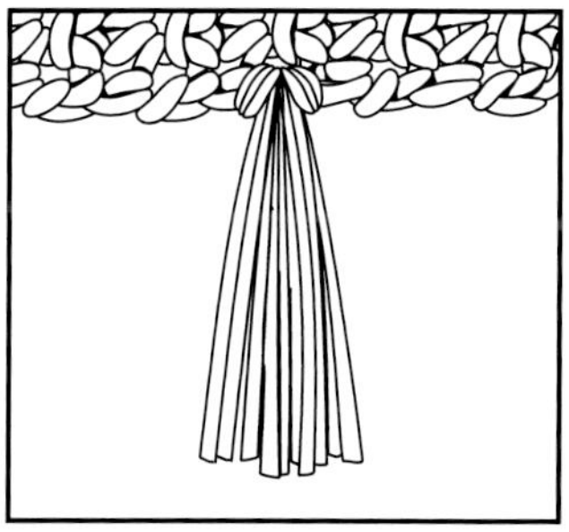

YARN INFORMATION

The Afghans in this leaflet were made using Sport Weight, Worsted Weight, or Bulky Weight Yarn. Any brand of Sport Weight, Worsted Weight, or Bulky Weight Yarn may be used. It is best to refer to the yardage/meters when determining how many balls or skeins to purchase. Remember, to arrive at the finished size, it is the GAUGE/TENSION that is most important, not the brand of yarn.

For your convenience, listed below are the specific yarns used to create our photography models.

ANGELS AMONG US
Red Heart® TLC® Essentials
White - #2101 White
Blue - #2816 Powder Blue

BABY'S BEST BLANKIE
Bernat® Softee® Baby
White - #2000 White
Green - #2004 Mint
Pink - #2001 Pink

CLOWN CARNIVAL
Red Heart® Kids
Blue - #2845 Blue
White - #2001 White
Red - #2390 Red
Yellow - #2230 Yellow
Orange - #2252 Orange
Green - #2677 Green
Black - #2012 Black

DOUBLE-TAKE
Red Heart® Classic
Dk Plum - #533 Dark Plum
Plum - #531 Lt Plum
Lt Lavender - #579 Lt Lavender
Variegated - #997 Sage Mary

ENCHANTED LACE
Red Heart® TLC® Essentials
#2101 White

FLOWERS FOR THOUGHT
Bernat® Berella® "4"®
Ecru - #8940 Natural
Green - #1232 Gentle Green
Blue - #1142 True Periwinkle Blue
Gold - #8887 Pale Tapestry Gold
Rose - #8814 Pale Antique Rose

GLIMPSE OF GRANNY
Red Heart® Soft
White - #7001 White
Green - #7672 Lt Yellow Green
Purple - #7582 Lt Amethyst
Teal - #7502 Lt Teal

HANDMADE HEARTS
Red Heart® Soft
Ecru - #7313 New Aran
Rose - #7772 Lt Country Rose
Green - #7672 Lt Yellow Green

INCREDIBLE IN WHITE
Red Heart® TLC® Essentials
#2101 White

JAZZY JOURNEY
Lion Brand® Jiffy®
Lt Green - #156 Mint
Green - #181 Country Green

KID'S PLAY
Red Heart® Kids
White - #2001 White
Red - #2390 Red
Green - #2677 Green
Blue - #2845 Blue
Yellow - #2230 Yellow

LAP OF LUXURY
Red Heart® TLC® Essentials
#2220 Butter

MILE-A-MINUTE MAGIC
Caron Perfect Match®
Blue - #7708 Slate Blue
Dk Blue - #7736 Cape Cod Blue
White - #7702 Winter White

NO-NONSENSE ACCENTS
Red Heart® Super Saver®
Black - #312 Black
Yellow - #320 Cornmeal
Rose - #375 Raspberry
Blue - #347 Lt Periwinkle
Teal - #359 Medium Teal

ONE-OF-A-KIND
Lion Brand® Homespun®
Ecru - #309 Deco
Blue - #302 Colonial

PERFECTLY PIECED

Red Heart® Soft
Tan - #7335 Camel
Ecru - #7313 New Aran
Black - #7012 Black

QUIET QUEST

Red Heart® TLCt®
Ecru - #5017 Natural
Black - #5012 Black
Brown - #5339 Mushroom
Orange - #5289 Copper

RAINBOW FOR BABY

Red Heart® Super Saver®
White - #311 White
Pink - #724 Baby Pink
Peach - #325 Peach
Yellow - #322 Pale Yellow
Green - #363 Pale Green
Blue - #381 Lt Blue

SPRING SERENADE

Red Heart® Soft
White - #7001 White
Teal - #7502 Lt Teal

TINY TWIRLS

Red Heart® Super Saver®
Ecru - #313 Aran
Purple - #579 Pale Plum
Pink - #372 Rose Pink
Yellow - #320 Cornmeal
Green - #661 Frosty Green

UNIVERSAL APPEAL

Red Heart® Super Saver®
Black - #312 Black
Scrap Colors:
#364 Lt Mint
#322 Pale Yellow
#327 Lt Coral
#375 Raspberry
#384 Skipper Blue
#388 Teal
#358 Lavender
#774 Lt Raspberry
#353 Lilac

Red Heart® Classic
Scrap Color: #683 Lt Seafoam

VISION IN BLACK

Red Heart® Super Saver®
Variegated - #303 Painted Desert Print
Black - #312 Black

WONDERFULLY ORIGINAL

Red Heart® Super Saver®
Lt Blue - #382 Country Blue
Blue - #380 Windsor Blue
Tan - #334 Buff
Brown - #336 Warm Brown

XTRA EASY

Red Heart® Super Saver®
Black - #312 Black
Off-White - #313 Aran
Burgundy - #376 Burgundy
Green - #631 Lt Sage
Yellow - #320 Cornmeal

YEN FOR YO-YOS

Red Heart® Super Saver®
Black - #312 Black
Scrap Colors:
#358 Lavender
#364 Lt Mint
#375 Raspberry
#320 Cornmeal
#359 Med Teal
#327 Lt Coral
#353 Lilac
#774 Lt Raspberry

ZEAL FOR ZIG-ZAGS

Bernat® Berella® "4"®
Black - #8994 Black
Rose - #1505 Dk Country Rose
Brown - #1012 True Taupe
Tan - #1011 Soft Taupe
Green - #1242 Deep Forest Green
Peach - #1507 Soft Peach

Production Team:
Instructional Editor - Sue Galucki;
Technical Editor - Cathy Hardy;
Artist - Faith Lloyd;
Senior Artist - Diana Sanders;
Photo Stylist - Janna Laughlin;
Photographer - Russ Ganser.

Afghans made and instructions tested by Janet Akins, Anitta Armstrong, Belinda Baxter, Pam Bland, Mike Cates, Marianna Crowder, Freda Gillham, Linda Graves, Jean Hall, Kay Meadors, Dale Potter, Clare Stringer, Carol Thompson, and Mary Valen.